PENGUIN BOOKS
THE FLY TRAP

Fredrik Sjöberg collects hoverflies on the island of Runmarö, in the
archipelago east of Stockholm. He is also a literary critic, translator,
cultural columnist and the author of several books including *The Art
of Flight* and *The Raisin King*, which form a trilogy with *The Fly Trap*.

Fredrik Sjöberg

The Fly Trap

Translated by Thomas Teal

PENGUIN BOOKS

PENGUIN BOOKS

UK | USA | Canada | Ireland | Australia
India | New Zealand | South Africa

Penguin Books is part of the Penguin Random House group of companies
whose addresses can be found at global.penguinrandomhouse.com.

Penguin
Random House
UK

First published by Particular Books 2014
Published in Penguin Books 2015
001

Copyright © Fredrik Sjöberg, 2014
Translation copyright © Thomas Teal, 2015

The moral right of the author and translator has been asserted

Set in Bembo Book 11.5/18 pt by Palimpsest Book Production Limited, Falkirk, Stirlingshire
Printed in Great Britain by Clays Ltd, St Ives plc

A CIP catalogue record for this book is available from the British Library

978-1-846-14778-4

www.greenpenguin.co.uk

Penguin Random House is committed to a
sustainable future for our business, our readers
and our planet. This book is made from Forest
Stewardship Council® certified paper.

Contents

There are only three subjects: love, death and flies. Ever since man was invented, this emotion, this fear and the presence of these insects have been his constant companions. Other people can take care of the first two subjects. Me, I just concern myself with flies – a much greater theme than men, though maybe not greater than women.

Augusto Monterroso, *Hispianola (Addendum)*

Chapter 1

The Curse of the Starving Class

It was during the time I wandered the streets near Nybroplan with a lamb in my arms. I remember it so well. Spring had come. The air was dry, almost dusty. The evening was chilly but still carried the smell of earth and last year's leaves, warmed by the sun. The lamb bleated forlornly as I crossed Sibyllegatan.

During the day, the animal lived with the king's pampered horses in the Royal Stables, down towards Strandvägen, and we understood that it must feel out of place, not only there but also, in the evenings, at the theatre. I know nothing about lambs, but old it was not. A few weeks, maybe. Playing the part of a living metaphor on stage must have been an ordeal, especially since the play – Sam Shepard's American drama *Curse of the Starving Class* – was violent in places, and noisy, and hard to digest, even for full-grown human beings. We could only hope that the poor creature was able to just grit its teeth and think about something else. In any case, it grew, faster than anyone had reckoned on.

And now, once and for all, that was my problem. A foggy mixture of ambition and coincidence had led me to a job at the Royal Dramatic Theatre, and for the past couple of years I had been in the properties department, responsible for taking care of often rather peculiar props for various productions, so it fell to me to fetch the unhappy animal from the Royal Stables before every performance. I carried it in my arms. We undoubtedly made a sweet picture in the spring evening. And then when the curtain rose, the lamb (later the sheep) was to make its periodic entrances and exits, keep quiet, and preferably not soil the stage, all with the scrupulous precision of any other scenery change. In pitch darkness.

Before the opening, while we were still in rehearsal,

we planned a mechanical lamb, a woolly stuffed animal with a movable head and a built-in speaker that would deliver adorable bleats at exactly the right moment by simply having the stage manager press a button. But when the director saw our expensive robot, he thought it over for about four seconds before condemning the attempt as futile. If the stage directions specified a real lamb, then we would have a real lamb, not a toy. So that was that. The lamb became my responsibility. And that is how it came about that spring that I began to ask myself what I thought I was doing, and why.

Now you may well wonder what a young entomologist was doing in the theatre in the first place. It is indeed a troubling question, one I'd rather not dig into too deeply. Anyway, it was a long time ago. Let's just say that he wanted to impress the girls, an area where entomologists need all the help they can get. Or it might be better to say that all of us need to flee blindly from time to time so as not to become copies of the world's expectations, and maybe, too, to give us the courage to remember some of those great, bold

3

thoughts that made a child get up in the night, heart pounding, and write down a secret promise for his life.

In any case, it was an exciting job. Fascinating and attractive to an outsider. Nothing can swallow fear head first like a large theatre in a strange city; nothing is more intoxicating than the dreams that dwell in its walls. Of course there was much that I never understood about the tricks of the playwright's trade or the unwritten subtext in a manuscript, the subtleties and tiny footnotes. But it didn't bother me, not to begin with.

Ingmar Bergman had returned from Munich, and it was all a great celebration. Shakespeare was mounted on the main stage in a great hubbub of activity, and those of us who padded quietly along the fly galleries and in the wings were able to transform the smallest glimpse of the master into anecdotes about his whims and legendary magic touch – small, plain stories that got better and bolder in the city's bars and could easily be turned into envy of and interest in the storyteller himself. Gogol rolled in like an armoured cruiser, and Norén ground down all resistance even from the most obdurate audiences. Strindberg, Molière, Chekhov. My relation to all of this was perhaps looser than that of the younger stagehands, property mistresses, dressers, extras and assistants with unclear assignments with whom the theatre teems — looser because almost all of them wanted to become famous actors and actresses themselves and stand in the spotlight, so they suffered mightily from their longing and from other people's success and from the capricious rule of theatre-school auditions.

The work was rarely demanding. You followed a production from the first rehearsals until the play closed. In the beginning, it was about understanding the director and even more so the set designer, which is an art in itself. Then later you rehearsed scene changes with the cast and crew and checked the props as they arrived from the warehouse and workshops. By the time of the opening, we usually had everything down pat.

But this particular play was different. It was not just that the increasingly unmanageable lamb was a constant source of concern. It was also a food play, by which I mean that food was prepared on stage. There are several fairly simple ways of dealing with this problem, but certain directors and designers always want to make things difficult. That is to say, if the actors are supposed to cook a meal, then they have to cook a meal. No substitutes. Of course you can use apple juice for cognac and beer. But the food has to be real. In this case, they were supposed to sauté some kidneys. The smell of frying kidneys fills a theatre in no time at all, which it was felt added a certain authenticity.

When the lights went out for scene changes, we prop people rushed in like silverfish across a bathroom floor to rearrange the furniture, clear the table, set the table, carry a lot of stuff in and out – in this case, among other things, a wheelbarrow, a broken door and innumerable artichokes. During one of these pitch-black scene changes it was thus our job – with the aid of nothing but memory and tiny luminous strips of tape on the stage floor – to place raw kidneys into a frying pan on a stove of the type supposed to have stood in American rural kitchens in the 1950s. The number of seconds allotted for this task was precise and verged on the impossible. And as if that weren't enough, *Curse of the Starving Class* had another curious feature – we can call it technical – which I would guess is unique in the history of Swedish theatre.

The thing was that in one particular scene, Wesley, the son in the family, played by Peter Stormare, was to show his contempt for his younger sister's vapid life by pissing on some charts she had made at a scout meeting.

So the workshop was instructed to construct a gadget with which to simulate this act, and shortly before opening night it appeared – a device, ingenious in its simplicity, consisting of a tube and a rubber bladder. The trouble was merely that the director, at this delicate juncture in the play, placed Stormare far downstage, facing the audience. This created a serious credibility problem. And when it then became clear that the gadget leaked so badly that Wesley appeared to suffer from incontinence, there occurred what I had already begun to fear.

'Oh, what the hell,' Stormare said. 'I'll just pee.' And so he did.

My artistic sense was still rather undeveloped, but

I was nevertheless deeply impressed by this unusual ability, night after night, month after month, to realize the playwright's vision and the director's weakness for unusual effects by very calmly urinating on stage just a few feet from the noses of the very cultivated ladies in the first row. What a gift! Naturally it was only a matter of time before he wound up in Hollywood, where he won undying fame as the silent, psychopathic kidnapper in *Fargo*.

Where I would wind up was less certain, but because it was I and I alone who was entrusted with the task of cleaning up this example of great acting – on my knees, in the dark, with a rag, hastily – it became clearer and clearer to me that my place was not, perhaps, in the theatre.

I may be exaggerating everything that happened in those days, romanticizing my longing and my fear, remembering only occasional lines of dialogue. It's possible, I know, but it was definitely spring and I was absolutely both confused and in love. On top of which, certain lines stuck to me like birthmarks. Not because they meant so very much, not then, but maybe just because they matched the colour of something in my life.

When Wesley stands downstage and disgraces himself, and his mother Ella has just complained about the way he's only making everything worse for his poor sister, he says, 'I'm not. I'm opening up new possibilities for her. Now she'll have to do something else. It could change her whole direction in life. She'll look back and remember the day her brother pissed all over her charts and see that day as a turning point in her life.'

That happened in the first act. In the third, when the sister finally leaves and makes his words prophetic, she bursts out, 'I'm gone. I'm gone. Never to return.'

I used to repeat those very words to myself, quietly but with the same rebellious tone used on stage, when, late at night, I returned to the stables with my shaggy friend from the country. Later that spring, I could no longer carry the lamb, so I led it on a leash, like a dog of some breed unknown even in snooty Östermalm. Elderly ladies stared after us, but we paid no attention and went on forging our plans in silence.

Only one year later, I lived here on the island – along

with the girl who sat in the audience one evening and said later that the play was both funny and moving, yet wrapped in a singular fragrance of wool, piss and sautéed kidney. That was 1985. I was twenty-six years old. All this business with flies – that too was only a matter of time.

Chapter 2

My Entry into Hoverfly High Society

The theatre was my second attempt to flee from entomology. Aimless travel was the first. And I am, of course, painfully aware of how sorry a subject can seem when the only approach to it is flight. But that's the truth, and there's no way around it.

No sensible person is interested in flies, or anyway no woman. At least not yet, I like to think, although in the end I'm always quite happy that no one else cares. The competition isn't exactly murderous. And when all is said and done, what I wanted to be best at was not urinating before an audience – my nerves were too delicate for that – but something else, anything at all actually, and finally it became obvious that my talents lay with flies.

That's a fate that takes some getting used to.

Anyway, the hoverflies are only props. No, not only, but to some extent. Here and there, my story is about something else. Exactly what, I don't know. Some days I tell myself that my mission is to say something about the art and sometimes the bliss of limitation. And the legibility of landscape. Other days are more dismal. As if I were queueing in the rain outside confessional literature's nudist colony, mirrors everywhere, blue with cold.

But as I now live on an island in the sea and am not an expert on anything but hoverflies, we will simply have to start there. Should someone have the desire, or simply the kindhearted impulse, they could bind it all together in the genre – mostly unknown in Sweden – so lovingly practised by the Smiths, Ken and Vera, in their quite fabulous book *A Bibliography of the Entomology of the Smaller British Offshore Islands*. It wouldn't be easy to do, I'm afraid, but after all it's the thought that counts.

In my library, which is large enough to withstand

a Russian siege, this book occupies a unique position. It is quite thin, just over one hundred pages, light blue in colour, and it has perhaps taught me little more than that Englishmen are crazy, but I am always equally exhilarated when I see it, heft it in my hand and read its title, as if it somehow justifies my existence. The text on the back of the dust jacket tells how the authors met and fell in love at Keele University in 1954 and how, later, they began studying flies together and started to collect literature about the insects on smaller islands. The couple are pictured as well, separately, and I can assure you that they look very nice. Ken – thin-haired, dressed in a suit, waistcoat and tie – seems to be hiding an ironic smile in his neatly trimmed beard, while Vera looks a little as if she had just woken up, with rosy cheeks. She appears to be thinking about something else. You can see that he loves her.

The book consists of a long list, nothing else. A catalogue of every known book and article about insect fauna on the islands along the coasts of Great Britain, from Jersey in the south to the Shetland Islands in the north. More than a thousand titles.

What is it these people have tried to capture? Hardly just insects.

. . .

In short, my artistic sense remained relatively undeveloped, and my past, as always, caught up with me. When anyone asked, therefore, I said succinctly that hoverflies are meek and mild creatures, easy to collect, and that they appear in many guises. Sometimes they don't even look like flies. Some of them look like hornets, others like honeybees, parasitic ichneumon wasps, gadflies or fragile, thin-as-thread mosquitoes so tiny that normal people never even notice them. Several species resemble large, bristly bumblebees, complete with in-flight drone and coats flecked with pollen. Only the expert is not deceived. We are not many, but we grow very old.

Nevertheless, the differences are great, in fact greater than the similarities. For example, wasps and bumblebees, like all the other hymenoptera, have four wings, whereas flies have only two. That's elementary. But it's a thing people seldom see, principally because flies can easily achieve several hundred wing beats per second.

The entomological literature that soon began to fill my island house tells of a Finnish scientist named Olavi Sotavalta, whose interests included an investigation of insect wing frequencies. In particular, he occupied himself with the biting midges, which manage to reach an astonishing frequency of 1,046 wing beats per second. Sophisticated instruments in his laboratory allowed him to measure exactly and unambiguously, but just as important for Sotavalta's research was his wonderful musicality and the fact that he had perfect pitch. He could determine the frequency simply by listening to the hum, and the foundation of his renown was laid when, in a famous experiment, he managed to trim the wings of a midge in order to increase the frequency beyond the limits of what seemed possible. He warmed up the midge's tiny body several degrees above normal and cut its wings with a scalpel to minimize air resistance, whereupon the little beast achieved no less than 2,218 wing beats per second. It was during the war.

In my mind's eye, I see Olavi Sotavalta lying on

his back in his grey-green sleeping bag somewhere in the bright summer nights of northernmost Finland, maybe on the shore of Lake Inari, smiling to himself as he listens to billions of hums from the space around him, thin as filaments of mica.

But I was going to talk about disguises, about the art of mimicking a bumblebee. We all know why. Profitability. Birds like to eat flies but usually avoid hymenoptera, which can sting. And so nature's perpetual arms race has formed masses of harmless flies into lifelike reproductions of all sorts of unpleasant things. I don't know why hoverflies have become such superb impostors, but that's what's happened, just as surely as the sun was shining from a clear blue high-summer sky one day when, at the very beginning of my career as a fly expert, I stood on watch in a clump of bishop's weed in bloom. There were insects everywhere. Pearl butterflies, rose-chafers, longhorn beetles, bumblebees, flies, all sorts. And me, of course, wearing shorts and a sunhat, armed with the blissful thoughtlessness of the trigger-happy hunter and a short-shafted, collapsible tulle net of Czech design.

Then, suddenly, a coal black missile came in from the right two metres above the nettles. I had just enough time to think 'stone bumblebee', no more, but within a fraction of a second I also thought I sensed a strange lightness of behaviour. Very subtle, barely perceptible, but the very suspicion released a reflex backhand sweep of my net.

That catch came to be my ticket of admission into hoverfly high society.

But first, a more comprehensive setting of the scene. We'll need to take this from the top. And what better place to start than with a description of how the hunt takes place. We are all familiar with the conventional image of the entomologist as a breathless twit rushing wildly across fields and meadows in pursuit of swiftly fleeing butterflies. Quite aside from the fact that this image is not entirely true to life, I can assure you that it is utterly incorrect when it comes to collectors of hoverflies. We are quiet, contemplative people, and our behaviour in the field is relatively aristocratic. Running is not necessarily beneath our dignity, but it is in any case pointless because the flies move much too fast. Consequently, we stand still, as if on guard, and moreover almost exclusively in places with blazing sunshine, little breeze and fragrant flowers. Passers-by can therefore easily get the impression that the fly hunter is a convalescent of some kind, momentarily lost in meditation. This is not wholly inaccurate.

The equipment is not remarkable. Net in one hand, pooter in the other. The latter is a sucking device consisting of a short, transparent fibreglass cylinder with corks at both ends. A plastic tube runs through one of the corks and a long hose through the other. The tube is pointed carefully at sitting flies, the hose is held in the user's mouth. And if he can get close enough without scaring the fly, a quick intake of breath is all it takes to suck it into the fibreglass cylinder. A fine-meshed filter in the rear cork prevents the animal from continuing on down his throat. Answering constant impertinent questions about his sanity is, however, unpreventable. Believe me, I have heard every conceivable insinuation and witticism along these lines. So I know from experience that the only way to cool off the grinning idiots is with an unexpected demonstration of the third piece of equipment – the poison bottle.

With the casual ease of a man of the world, I haul it out of my pocket and remark, truthfully, that I have in my hand enough cyanide to put the entire population of the island to sleep for good. All the cheap grins are then promptly transformed into respectful questions about how in hell a person gets his hands on cyanide, which I never reveal. Many experts use ethyl acetate, others chloroform, but I prefer cyanide. It's more effective.

Almost three hundred people live on the island.

The big black fly flapped about and died quickly in the poison fumes, and since this occurred during my first summer of fly catching (we had then lived on the island for ten years), I didn't know right away what species I had captured. I could see it was a hoverfly, that's something you learn in a few days, but it was only later that day, at the microscope, surrounded by teetering stacks of books with titles like *British hoverflies*, *Danmarks svirrefluer* and *Biologie der Schwebfliegen*

Deutschlands, that I realized it was a rare *Criorhina ranunculi*.

The very next morning, for the first time, the island received a visit from the country's foremost expert on the *Syrphidae*, the hoverfly family. He examined my trophy sceptically but then brightened up, questioned me at length about the place of capture, congratulated me, and then, over coffee, related the following history.

Of all the hoverflies in the country, *Criorhina ranunculi* is not only one of the largest and most beautiful, it is also so rare that in the early 1990s the decision was made to list it as extinct in Sweden. At that time, it had not been seen for sixty years. The total number of sightings was three: two in Östergötland and one in Småland.

My newfound friend paused for effect and poured a dollop of milk into his coffee cup. The swifts cried, a great loon was fishing out beyond the dock, and far away I could hear taxi boats in the strait that divides the island from the mainland. It was a hot July day.

The species was seen for the first time in 1874, in Gusum in the province of Östergötland. The man holding the net was no less a personage than Peter Wahlberg, the man who succeeded Berzelius in the post of Permanent Secretary of the Royal Academy of Science in the eventful year 1848. After a long life in the service of research as a botanist and professor of *materia medica* at the Karolinska Institute, he had now worked his way up to flies, which strikes me as reasonable and logical considering the fact that back in 1833 he was one of the founders of the Society for the Spread of Useful Knowledge, later dissolved. He was probably a happy man. His portrait in the encyclopaedia suggests as much. His younger brother, on the other hand, looks mostly angry, as if he suffered from toothache or poor finances. His name was Johan Wahlberg and he was more the adventurous type, known to posterity as an African explorer, big game hunter and manic collector of articles of natural history. He died before his time in a fight with an elephant.

The next time *Criorhina ranunculi* turned up was in Korsberga on the Småland plateau. That was in 1928, the collector was Daniel Gaunitz, and four years later another specimen was caught in Borensberg by his brother Sven, later the author of a series of informative articles including 'The Old-House Borer in Mariefred' and 'Coprophiles of Åtvidaberg'. There was a third brother, too, named Carl Bertil. They came from Sorsele. All of them wrote books, mostly about insects.

Anyway, after Borensberg, *Criorhina ranunculi* vanished for a generation, until the man across the table from me on the terrace managed to find a couple of specimens on the western outskirts of Stockholm. My fly was in any case the sixth one ever seen in Sweden. It was my first triumph. Since then, I and others have seen the species many times, either because it has become more common or, more likely, because we have learned more about which flowers it visits, and when, and what kind of rotting deciduous trees its larvae cannot easily survive without. And how to distinguish it from a stone bumblebee.

The real difficulty turned out to be explaining my happiness to the uninitiated.

In his short story 'The Man Who Loved Islands', D. H. Lawrence writes:

The years were blending into a soft mist, from which nothing obtruded. Spring came. There was never a primrose on his island, but he found a winter aconite. There were two little sprayed bushes of blackthorn, and some wind-flowers. He began to make a list of the flowers on his islet, and that was absorbing. He noted a wild currant bush, and watched for the elder flowers on a stunted little tree, then for the first yellow rags of the broom, and wild roses. Bladder campion, orchids, stitchwort, celandine, he was prouder of them than if they had been people on his island. When he came across the golden saxifrage, so inconspicuous in a damp corner, he crouched over it in a trance, he knew not for how long, looking at it. Yet it was nothing to look at. As the widow's daughter found, when he showed it her.

Chapter 3

A Trap in Rangoon

Many years ago, before the island and the theatre, I took a passenger barge up the mighty Congo River. What an adventure! What stories I would tell! About freedom! But it didn't happen. I never managed to say much more than that the forests were vast and the river as broad as Kalmar Sound. And that I'd been there. So it goes when you travel for the sake of something to say. Your eyes go weak. All I could have written were endless disquisitions about homesickness. So I kept my mouth shut.

It's a different story with Ladäng Creek, I thought aloud to myself one morning among the bird-cherry blossoms. Then something remarkable happened.

I was in the process of rigging up my big California fly trap between a couple of over-blooming sallow bushes down by the creek – a complicated manoeuvre – when suddenly a complete stranger appeared as if from nowhere. He just stepped straight out of the lush June greenery and addressed me politely and apologetically in English. A wood warbler sang its silver song somewhere in the trembling crown of a nervous aspen, and a pike splashed in the shallow water of the creek. The mosquitoes were stubborn in the shade. He said it was me he was looking for.

'I'm looking for you,' were his exact words.

I tried to accept this as the most natural thing in the world, as if strangers could be expected to seek me out wherever I might be. But I failed completely. Instead I stood there like an idiot among the sedge tussocks, amazed and speechless.

This man was in fact, and still is, the only person I've ever encountered by Ladäng Creek. If you want to be left in peace, it's a good place to go. Islanders never go there, and the summer people don't know the place exists. The paths that once led there have now vanished.

The name of the creek is not even on the map. For that matter, it's not much of a waterway, more of a ditch – overgrown, silted up and periodically dry. The meadow barns that are said to have stood there are long gone, as indeed are the meadows. Slowly but surely they've been invaded by fir, aspen, birch and alder. All the same, it's a very pretty place, as rich and spacious as a cathedral when the marsh marigolds bloom in the spring. Deer meet down by the creek, sometimes moose, but never people. Except that day.

In the Middle Ages, Ladäng Creek was the channel boats used to sail to a village at the far end of the bay which rising land elevations eventually turned into a fresh-water lake. The village is still there. It's where we live. How old it is no one knows, but there were probably people living here as early as Viking times. The inner parts of the long bay, where the humus-brown water is very deep, must have made an ideal harbour – a sanctuary that seafarers with base intentions surely hesitated to venture into. The granite cliff drops straight into the water. The village was easily defended against attackers from the open ocean to the east.

What ships anchored here outside my window? Who rowed up the creek where today a pike can hardly make its way?

'I'm looking for you.'

Who had told him I would be right here? How very strange. Why hadn't he called first, as other people do, or at least sent a letter or an email saying he wanted to arrange a meeting? A fly person, of course. News travels fast and globally in our line of work. *Criorhina ranunculi* has not yet been observed in England, and *Blera fallax* is a rarity, a fabulous creature that collectors there can only dream about. Here it is not uncommon. There is no shortage of reasons. It struck me that maybe it was my seven specimens of *Doros profuges* that explained my standing here eye to eye with a fully equipped Englishman, complete with an oilskin coat of that indeterminate colour favoured by military quartermasters. Middle-aged, balding, foolishly bare-headed, waving his arms like a semaphore.

As mentioned earlier, the mosquitoes were annoying.

But in that case, I thought, he's come way too

early. *Doros* doesn't appear until the first week in July. If we're lucky, that is. Sometimes it never appears at all.

The Englishman then initiated a conversation that gradually dispelled my questions – and left me embarrassed at my own presumption. But to start with, the whole thing grew even stranger. He stepped towards me across the mud with a book in his hand that quickly revealed itself to be a well-thumbed copy of *Stockholmstraktens Växter*, a guide to the plant life of the Stockholm region, published in 1912. As if it were a perfectly natural continuation of his puzzling opening remark, he approached me eagerly with the book opened to a page showing local trees. And it was only then that I realized it wasn't me he was looking for, and that what he had said was not 'I'm looking for you', but rather 'I'm looking for yew', a tree that, according to his guidebook, grew 'abundantly' on this island.

I've run into any number of strange botanists over the years. It's usually orchids they're searching for – lady's slippers, red helleborine, marsh helleborine. And they get lost. Especially if what they're looking for is white adder's mouth, not to mention the musk orchid, which no one has seen on the island since 1910, when Sten Selander, a botanist and member of the Swedish Academy, found a single specimen. I have answered their questions, sometimes a little evasively in order to save the orchids from getting trampled to extinction, but this one was new. So when I had told the man where the island's yews might be found, I ventured to ask how it was that his curiosity had taken such an unexpected turn this lovely summer day.

'Why yew?'

'Well, you see,' he said, and went on to explain quite openly that he was freelancing for a French pharmaceutical company that had assigned him to investigate this and other areas of Northern Europe for the possibility of harvesting taxol, a substance found in the inner bark of the yew, which has shown itself to be an amazingly effective agent against various forms of cancer. I knew quite a bit about taxol from a book I had translated – enough to have quite a satisfactory conversation about it. Moreover, I could tell him with great certainty that the yews here on the island were too few and too frail to be of use. He was looking for large stands. There were none here. The Baltic States might be worth a look, I suggested. (It was just a guess, plucked from thin air.) The man listened attentively as he waved his arms. Yes, he was on his way in that direction. By way of Gotland, if I understood him correctly. Then we talked for a bit about ferries and about the weather before he thanked me for my help and walked on, to the southeast, towards the limestone outcroppings by the mouth of the creek. An odd man. And the last thing he said was as remarkable as the first.

'By the way, it's a large one, your Malaise trap.'

Say what you like about Englishmen, but they are often cultured people. In the course of our brief conversation, we had not touched upon what I was doing there in the undergrowth by the creek. We had not said a word about insects. Of course he had noticed my hand net, but unlike all my fellow Swedes, he had clearly seen it as no more than a perfectly natural part of what a gentleman is expected to carry with him when wandering field and forest. He had not felt the need to ask questions. How pleasant! His comment about the trap was merely an acknowledgement. He did not ask what it was, not even if it *was* a Malaise trap. Simply observed in passing that it was large.

That was the last thing he said. And I stood there in the sedge, as noted earlier, quite speechless.

. . .

The point is that he was right. My fly trap is American and for that reason so disproportionately large that my friends on the mainland were under the impression that I had purchased a party tent. The model, called the Mega Malaise Trap, is six metres wide and three metres high. In addition, it has double collecting vessels. A real monster. A more effective trap does not exist.

For a long time, I wouldn't hear of it. In the early years, I was openly hostile to traps of every kind. There was something unsportsmanlike about them, something greedy, and moreover it seemed to me that anyone reduced to using a trap was missing the more poetic dimensions of fly collecting – anticipation, repose and slowness.

'I'm no industrialist', was my usual reply when asked why I didn't get myself a Malaise trap. I didn't even like to use yellow pan traps, that is to say, shallow yellow bowls of water in which flies drown because they're so dumb they think everything yellow is a flower. Even today I have a certain contempt for this simplest of all traps, which requires no talent, just patience in the sorting out of hymenoptera, beetles, butterflies, and all the other poor creatures that keep the flies company in this quickly disgusting soup of disappointed nectar seekers.

But however it happened, the Malaise trap began to excite my imagination. Wherever anyone deployed one, even if it was only on a marsh in the trackless wastes of Lapland, remarkable hoverflies turned up. So what might not turn up here? Species whose existence on the island I'd never dreamed of might allow themselves to be captured in this way, of that I was convinced. And since it was getting harder and harder to find new thrills, my resistance weakened. When you spend two weeks in a row standing like a statue in a spirea thicket without seeing hide nor hair of an unfamiliar hoverfly, you start to think. You think, for example, about the insects you're missing because they don't exist right here, right now, or because they just fly past like untouchable meteors. A Malaise trap, you think finally, might at least be an interesting experiment.

Once you've thought that far, you're a goner. In my case, I tried telling myself, just for fun, that a Malaise trap in the garden would simply be a belated tribute to one of my really great heroes.

Of course! It would be an act of reverence! Done and done.

René Malaise was born in 1892 and lived until 1978. He was Swedish, which few people realize. For entomologists all over the world, Malaise is a sort of free-floating concept – like Linnaeus – who stands above the limitations of national stereotype. There are innumerable insects bearing the species name *malaisei* in his honour, and his monograph on the taxonomy of southeast Asian sawflies – unreadable for the layperson, I'm sorry to say – is reputed to be unsurpassed. But fate decreed that his really fireproof fame would come to him not because of his research or his books or even his epic adventures, but rather because of an invention that was epoch-making in the truest sense of the word, an invention which, like so many ingenious innovations, was simple and seemed later to be obvious.

During one of his extensive journeys in foreign climes, he noticed that a great many insects found their way into his tent but never found their way out again, at least not the way they came in.

On one occasion, however, there was a small hole in one corner of the tent roof, and through this hole all the insects readily regained their freedom. And that gave René Malaise the impulse for his trap. He tells the story himself in an article printed in 1937 in *Entomologisk Tidskrift* (*Journal of Entomology*), written appropriately enough in English and with a classic opening line: 'Since the time of Linnaeus the technique of catching insects has not improved very much . . .' Unwarranted modesty was not, as far as one can tell, one of Malaise's distinguishing characteristics.

His observations from the wilderness had gradually crystallized into the idea of a gauzy arrangement of fine netting, not unlike an old-fashioned two-man tent with open sides. The peak of the roof sloped slightly upwards, and at its highest point there was a treacherous hole leading to an ingeniously constructed gas chamber. The prototype was constructed in Stockholm shortly before Malaise and his second (possibly third) wife headed off to the mountains and valleys of northern Burma to collect hymenoptera. The year was 1934, and the first five traps were sewn together in a tailor shop in Rangoon under the supervision of the inventor himself. Then they travelled north. The railroad ended at Myitkyina. With sixteen mules, they set course for the Chinese border.

Still today, scientists crouch over stereo microscopes sorting his collection. That's how effective his traps were. Over a few months, he and his wife captured well over 100,000 specimens, mostly of completely unknown species. Three-quarters of the sawflies – the group that Malaise himself studied – were new to science.

I have no idea what's new here on the island, and I don't care. There are certainly hundreds of unknown species – parasitic hymenoptera, fungal gnats and others – and many of them, probably, have already been caught in my net, but I'm interested only in hoverflies. There are, of course, some other groups that I'll collect for future use – jewel wasps, bee flies, wild bees, soldier flies – but I'd go crazy if I tried to include everything. For people like me, limits are an essential part of life. I too boarded the train in Rangoon once, but there's nothing more to tell. I got off in Mandalay and stayed for a week in a hotel. I remember a café, that's all.

In any case, once I'd given way to temptation, everything happened very quickly.

There are several makes of Malaise traps, some of them extremely handy, but since my decision was a defeat disguised as homage, I ordered the largest. Mega Malaise. From the USA. I absolutely believe that a certain person in his heaven smiled as I did so. I too was pleased with myself until I got a call from customs wondering what it was I had purchased from the mystical firm in California. They had unpacked the contraption and were now lost in thought. What in the world was this thing?

'A fly trap,' I said, foolishly.

At first there was complete silence, then a lot of questions about what I meant to use it for.

'Trapping flies,' I replied wittily. But I had aroused

the suspicion of the red-tape expert at the other end of the line and was then unable to make a successful case for classifying my rig under the heading 'Devices for Scientific Research'. As a result, an unreasonably heavy duty was assessed on the trap. Maybe I should have said it was a party tent. That would of course have been a lie, but only partly. I was in a party mood the very first night when I examined the collection chamber and found three hoverfly species that were new to the island, among them a specimen of *Chrysotoxum fasciatum* that to this day has never been seen here again.

All I did was hang up the trap between the woodshed and one corner of the house, and that's pretty much where it's stayed. Sometimes I manhandle it down to the creek or some other particularly promising place on the island, but for the most part it hangs out here in the garden. Every evening I put a couple of balls of tissue drenched in chloroform into the chamber, the same way southern European train robbers would knock a whole sleeping compartment senseless. Then I sort the booty and send my friend Malaise a mental note of thanks and admiration.

Where did he get the strength?

How did he manage to retain his sanity?

Sometimes I think it was simply a question of trust. He was secure in the knowledge that, come what may, this was his destiny. And he drew his strength from this certainty. He wrote very little, most of it now forgotten, but what there is seems to point in that direction.

One day as I stood looking for insects a short distance from the road, three men with large packs on their backs appeared. One of them was carrying a rifle, quite an unusual sight, as natives in Burma are forbidden to carry firearms. I had been watching these men from the moment they appeared around a crook in the road, but when the man with the rifle suddenly caught sight of me, he instantly raised the weapon and took aim. I had already realized that they must be opium smugglers. Had I made a careless movement, he would unquestionably have fired, but I relied on the fact that they must have heard about us and our insect gathering, so I turned my back and swung my net to catch an imaginary insect. I freely

admit that the next few seconds were tense, but when
I turned back a few moments later, all three men had
disappeared.

. . .

From time to time, I decide to get to the bottom of my reluctance to travel. Why am I such an unsuccessful globetrotter? Why am I so homesick all the time? The usual result of my efforts is that I just sit somewhere engulfed in a swarm of little, round, colourless thoughts that lack any perceptible coherence. As if some higher power had emptied its hole punch into my head.

Chapter 4

The Man Who Loved Islands

Towards the end of his brief life, D. H. Lawrence wrote a short story called 'The Man Who Loved Islands'. I had never read it, knew only its title, but I was nevertheless practically certain that the story would help me answer my eternally returning question: Why an island? For years I searched for this hard-to-find book in Stockholm's second-hand bookshops, although I felt no great urgency. The mere knowledge that Lawrence had got to the bottom of the riddle soothed me. The answer existed. Moreover, inevitably, I had theories of my own.

For even if this island is like a Sunday afternoon, fifteen square kilometres in size, it is nevertheless so small and isolated that everyone who chooses to settle here without having deep roots in the community is expected to explain the decision as if they were joining some peculiar sect. Always the same question. Why this island? And, as ever, love is a good answer – as all the women know who arrived from distant places and married into ancient island families by way of perennial homebody boys with greasy caps and shotguns – women who now run the island's practical and political affairs.

It's said to be the same all over the world, in all seven seas. Islands are matriarchies of a kind seldom seen on land. The men – as Iceland's president Vigdís Finnbogadóttir remarked on one occasion when the subject arose – the men flee to their own preferred landscape, which is the sea. They're simply not around. So it was and still is in places where fishing and piloting remain important. But here? No. Here something else is at work.

It is always something else. 'Circumstances.' Which is true, of course. And it makes a perfectly good answer, as does a longing for the raw beauty of the skerries and their shifting forms of silence at the edge of the open sea. Such things can be said, and in May, when the maples bloom and the rosefinch sings in the woods by the shore, no answers are needed, nor even questions. Nature is enough. Why *not* move out here? The change comes only later, several years later. It was only then that I thought I saw that the island had a peculiar attraction for men with a need for control and security, which they sought on land through power over others, but which out here was woven into the limitations of the insular landscape. For nothing is so enclosed and concrete as an island. In the old days, the days of seamen, the landscape was open and free in all directions. Now freedom takes a different form for those who find their way here. For us. For me.

Whichever way I go, sooner or later I come to the sea. That's a banal observation, but within it, I think, lies a security that for many islanders is greater than the feeling of being trapped. Maybe it's no more remark-able than sleeping better with the door closed. The thought struck me one summer morning when we had finally decided to capture the badger. Before it tipped over the house.

It usually lived under our cottage in the winter,

right under the floor, and as long as the children were little, we all thought the arrangement was exciting and congenial. The space was so small that we could sometimes hear the rough brush on his back rasping against the floorboards when he turned around in his winter sleep. It was only when we abandoned the old house and built a new one by the lake that we discovered that the foundation was so undermined by all the tunnels of his burrow that the building was about to collapse. There had to be a limit to our hospitality, so the next time the little wedge-nosed miscreant appeared and began to install himself under the cottage, we turned to one of those inscrutable men to be found on every island who always have a rancid bratwurst on hand with which to bait their galvanized badger-trap. This man set up his trap by the corner of the building. The very next morning, there lay the badger rolled up in a ball inside – sound asleep.

. . .

I need to interject here that the natives on our island are by no means exceptionally odd. Come to think of it, neither are the summer people. At least not compared with the new settlers, the enthusiasts who move out to the island, or anyway try to. Many come and leave again quickly, always with some equally idiotic project for which they're hoping to get a government grant, since the island is so sparsely populated that no project is too hare-brained to get official support.

People sometimes call me for help in investigating the possibilities. I am a biologist, after all. Their projects are often said to have an environmental dimension – the infallible key to getting grants – so I'm considered a good person to talk to. When we were new out here, I used to say that I was a writer, but all the women on the island felt so sorry for my wife that I started insisting I was a biologist instead. What else could I do? And if you're a biologist on an island widely known for its rich biosphere, you have to put up with a lot of phone calls from morons. They always seem to assume that I'm a moron myself.

One man called because he wanted to, as he put it, reconnoitre the island for a small-scale industrial initiative that ought to be a dream project for some

EU structural fund with the proper environmental orientation. He told me he'd been sitting at home one day watching the opening ceremony of some great sporting event – the Olympic Games, maybe, I don't remember exactly. Anyway there was a gigantic stadium and a brass band, a parade of national teams, speeches and acrobats. Buckets of polychrome metallic confetti had rained down like an April snow shower past the cameras flashing from the seats, and at that moment he was transformed from a couch potato into an entrepreneur.

His idea was very simple. He himself thought it was also brilliant. He was going to raise Brimstone butterflies. In humongous greenhouses, he would breed prodigious quantities of Brimstone larvae and then manipulate the pupation in a cooling chamber in order to somehow synchronize the emergence of the adult insects.

He was going to cripple the confetti industry by inducing tens of thousands of Brimstones to do something almost impossible to achieve with, say, three Peacock butterflies. That was his plan. He had seen hundreds of white doves released when events were launched on television. Bright yellow butterflies would be much prettier. 'You know, perfect.'

I told him the truth, that I thought his idea was just a tad optimistic, but that I would give a lot to see the result on a live broadcast, especially if it was raining. Thousands of butterflies floundering around on the grass, looking for something to hide under. It will make sports history, I said. He never called back. Neither did the genius who called to hear what I thought of the chances of leasing a little land on the island, which isn't hard to do. He wanted to start an organic horseradish farm, which didn't sound impractical either, I remarked. But to then sell it for the production of environmentally friendly tear gas to be used at riots? What was I supposed to say?

. . .

The man who loved islands was, of course, Lawrence himself, and the story was an allegory about his constant wandering among different cultures and philosophies. When I finally got my hands on the book, I was disappointed. Was this all? A man inclined to misanthropy buys an island intending to mould it to his own personality and make it his own world, but agriculture doesn't pay and his servants cheat him. So he sells the island and moves to a smaller one, with fewer servants and still fewer illusions, stands there in the wind and feels nothing, no joy, no longing, but has a child with the housekeeper's daughter, whereupon all desire dies within him with such sickening finality that he has to flee again, to a third island, just a rock in the roaring sea, where he loses his mind among lumpish, bleating sheep and finally freezes to death in his primitive shack. One of the man's final pleasures is that his cat vanishes and never reappears.

Only he still derived his single satisfaction from being alone, absolutely alone, with the space soaking into him. The grey sea alone, and the footing of his sea-washed island. No other contact. Nothing human to bring its horror into contact with him. Only space, damp, twilit, sea-washed space! This was the bread of his soul.

Frustrated, I stuffed the book back on the shelf and thought, this story is about neither islands nor love.

A couple of years later, I read it again, and then again, periodically, many times, especially when life on the island grew rigid from the pressure of encircling darkness and tragedy of a kind that the newcomer doesn't see. My first impression of that text no longer fit. Lawrence had seen something that on certain days I wanted to call true.

> *Out of the very air came a stony, heavy malevolence.*
> *The island itself seemed malicious. It would go on*
> *being hurtful and evil for weeks at a time. Then*
> *suddenly again one morning it would be fair, lovely*
> *as a morning in Paradise, everything beautiful and*
> *flowing. And everybody would begin to feel a great*
> *relief, and a hope for happiness.*

The parents in the story say that by living on the island they are not doing right by their children. Those who have no children feel they are not doing right by themselves. Yes, that's how it is, exactly.

But everything fell into place with the flies. In exercising control over something, however insignificant and apparently meaningless, there is a peaceful euphoria, however ephemeral and fleeting, which Lawrence manages to evoke when he has his alter ego on the islands recover his balance by means of more or less primitive botanical collecting. On the first island he seeks shelter in his well-filled library, where he is absorbed in endless labour on a book about all the flowers mentioned by the Greek and Latin writers of the ancient world. Later, on the second, smaller island, he fills his prison with a sometimes enthralling effort to compile a complete catalogue of all the plants on the island.

It is only on the third island that he loses all interest in botany. 'He was glad. He didn't want trees or bushes. They stood up like people, too assertive. His bare, low-pitched island in the pale blue sea was all he wanted.'

Buttonology is what it's called – disrespectful but accurate. As a collector, the man who loved islands is by disposition a classic buttonologist. He compiles catalogues. The idea is to be exhaustive, to include everything. In this way, the buttonologist differs from the mapmaker, whom he resembles and can easily be confused with. But the person who makes maps can never include everything in his picture of reality, which remains a simplification no matter what scale he chooses. Both attempt to capture something and to preserve it. And yet they are very different.

What bothers me is that on occasion the buttonologist, as in Lawrence's case, seems to be merely an erstwhile mapmaker, now well on his way to madness. It's just a phase.

Put a boy ashore on an islet and watch what happens. He'll charge around it. Every time. He bounds from stone to stone along the edge of the water like a happy animal, living proof that the word 'territorial' derives from the same root as 'terrier'. He's exploring his territory, following the coastline along its entire length like a cartographer, searching for driftwood and flotsam. Only then does he explore the interior of the island with the buttonologist's blessed tunnel vision.

Purple loosestrife sways in the light sea breeze. The heavy smell of seaweed. Arctic terns!

. . .

There are millions and millions of insect species here on earth. Of these, hundreds of thousands belong to the multifarious order of flies, *Diptera*. House flies, dance flies, robber flies, hoverflies, thick-headed flies, soldier flies, snipe flies, picture-winged flies, fruit flies, flesh flies, blowflies, stable flies, marsh flies, shore flies, louse flies, dung flies, parasite flies, stiletto flies – every imaginable name. In Sweden alone there are 4,424 different species, according to the most recent figures. New ones are discovered constantly.

Of all these very different fly families, I am interested only in hoverflies, also called flower flies. But even these are far too numerous to cover in the course of one lifetime, except superficially. Scientists have identified more than 5,000 hoverflies in the whole world, and there are undoubtedly thousands more that haven't yet been discovered or named, that simply exist God knows where. The 368 species of hoverfly found in Sweden to date are undeniably manageable. But our country is very large and verdant, and the days are so packed with impressions and clamorous information that I am forced to limit myself so as not to lose sight of something I am forever seeking.

Therefore I collect only on the island. Never on the mainland.

So far I have managed to capture 202 species. Two hundred and two.

A triumph, believe me. Only the difficulty of explaining is greater.

Not even on Öland or Gotland – those comparatively gigantic islands, where generations of entomologists have been capturing flies for all they're worth since the time of Linnaeus – not even there, over the course of a quarter of a millennium, have they managed to identify as many species as I have over the course of seven years here. The number says something about the island, and perhaps something about the depth of the buttonological pitfall, but most of all it says something about the possibilities of the sedentary life. When I get old, maybe I will pursue my hoverfly studies only in my own garden, sitting here in the sunshine by the meadowsweet and the butterfly bush like a caliph in his pleasure garden, the pooter hose in my mouth as if it led to an opium pipe.

Don't misunderstand me. We're talking about hunting for pleasure, nothing more. Of course I could name a number of very good, very sensible reasons why a person *ought* to collect flies. Scientific reasons, or environmental ones. And maybe I will, later, but it would be hypocritical to begin anywhere but with pure recreation. Anyway, I'm no missionary. Few collectors are. If anything, it's probably solitude that gets us to make up reasons that other people can understand. If I say that I collect hoverflies principally to map out changes in the local fauna, practically everyone will understand, even applaud, what I do. But it's a lie. Because enjoyment is so awkward. People who have not fallen into the trap themselves know nothing. On this point I am in agreement with Thomas De Quincey, who in *Confessions of an English Opium-Eater* dismisses all who believe they know something about the effects of intoxication on a restless soul.

[With regard to] all that has been hitherto written on the subject of opium, whether by travellers in Turkey (who may plead their privilege of lying as an old immemorial right) or by professors of medicine, writing ex cathedra, I have but one emphatic criticism to pronounce, – Lies! lies! lies!

He did in fact destroy himself with opium, completely. He sank so far that his broad interests during a particularly critical period were reduced to the study of the national economy, a subject which at that time was thought to be reserved for 'the very dregs and rinsings of the human intellect'. Of course he could also have confined himself to a description of the drawbacks, the misery of addiction, for there he was the greatest expert of them all – in precisely the same way that we entomologists can expand endlessly on the unpleasant effects of environmental devastation on the tiniest of creatures.

And nevertheless, the rapture of intoxication seeps in between the lines.

But, to quit this episode, and to return to my inter-
calary year of happiness. I have said already, that
on a subject so important to us all as happiness, we
should listen with pleasure to any man's experience or
experiments, even though he were but a ploughboy,
who cannot be supposed to have ploughed very deep
in such an intractable soil as that of human pains and
pleasures, or to have conducted his researches upon
any very enlightened principles.

Now, with the best will in the world, I cannot pretend
that I have ploughed very deeply into the soil of joy,
and into that of misery hardly at all, but however it
happened, I began to get a distinct feeling that René
Malaise had.

On a good day, his trap might give me a thousand
insects.

But that was only the beginning.

Chapter 5

The Archipelago of Buttonology

It was August Strindberg who coined the term button-ology. He was angry and needed a taunt. The old taunts wouldn't do, so he invented a new one – funnily enough in a short story called 'The Isle of the Blessed'. He wrote it in Switzerland in 1884 and, as usual, what he wanted was more than simple revenge for various injustices.

> *But because the idle found it difficult to do nothing, they invented every sort of idiotic foolishness. One began to collect buttons; a second gathered spruce, pine and juniper cones; a third procured a grant for travelling the world.*

Several years later he lived and wrote one of his best novels right here on the island, on the east side, facing the open sea. Yet I'm fairly certain he was not happy here. Eager as he was to conquer territories on a European order of magnitude – or larger – he belonged by natural necessity to the mainland. Finding peace in a little cage was not for him, it made him aggressive and ornery. It was here too, on Midsummer Day 1891, that he attacked his wife's Danish lover Marie David so violently that he was later hauled before the district court and found guilty of assault. 'Terrier' is still related to 'territory'.

The target of his innovative taunt in 'The Isle of the Blessed' is said to have been the archaeologist Oscar Montelius and his then famous typological method for establishing the chronology of bronze-age artifacts, but this has not prevented generations of ignorant wiseacres from applying Strindberg's characterization to other scientific systematizers, entomologists among them.

The man who collected buttons had accumulated a fearful quantity. As he did not know how he was going to preserve them, he sought and received money from the state to erect a building to house the collection. He then sat down to organize his buttons. There were many different ways of sorting them. One could divide them by garment – underwear buttons, trouser buttons, coat buttons, etc. – but our man devised a more artificial and therefore more difficult system. But to achieve this, he needed help. First he wrote a treatise on The Need for a Study of Buttons on Scientific Principles. Then he petitioned the Treasury for a Professorship in Buttonology, along with two assistants. His application was approved, more for the sake of creating employment than for the intrinsic value of the proposal, which no one was yet in a position to judge.

As usual, Strindberg works himself into a frenzy, heckling a society gone astray, in which cretinism and softening of the brain have taken on epidemic proportions. In the eyes of the volatile writer, the Kingdom of Sweden has become a stronghold of stupidity where ecclesiastical, artistic, scientific and political elites make war on one another with absolutely magnificent imbecility.

> *But the man who gathered cones, not wanting to come off second best, astonished the world with an enormous artificial system that divided all cones into 67 classes, 23 families and 1,500 orders.*

And, as a final proof that his fatherland was now in a state of spiritual distress, he tells us that the pompous men in power have now succeeded in persuading the oppressed masses that 'the state would collapse unless the people were prepared to grant a salary and professorship to a gentleman who had mounted a large number of bugs on zinc needles'.

· · ·

For a long time, I used the classic insect pins from Austria, but as my interest in hoverflies deepened, I switched to pins from the Czech Republic. They're cheaper. Otherwise there's no great difference. They're made of black enamelled steel, 40 millimetres long, with a little brass-yellow plastic head, and they come in seven sizes. The thickest is as stiff as a nail, while the thinnest, number 000, is as capricious and flexible as a French verb. You stick the pin right through the fly's thorax. That's all there is to it. For aesthetic reasons, you can use a couple of straight pins to spread the wings while they dry, but on the whole flies are very compliant collectibles. If you protect them in tight-fitting drawers from dermestid beetles and other misfortunes, they will last for several hundred years, which is a comforting thought for the entomologist.

About the drawers. The system was invented by a pedant but is nevertheless elegant. A lovely chest of large drawers full of small boxes under glass. The boxes, sixteen to a drawer, have no covers and can be moved around as new specimens are added or the old ones begin to overflow the banks. Suppose, for example, that one summer you decide to pin down a copious number of, say, *Brachyopa pilosa* in anticipation of the good time you'll have later, over the winter, as you examine them all under the microscope in hopes of finding a specimen of the very similar but infinitely rarer and in every way mysterious *Brachyopa obscura*. And when you've filled all your boxes with *Brachyopa*, you just put in a new box and push the others along. Quite simply the same principle as in that children's game where you move brightly coloured, hard plastic numbered tiles with your thumbs until you have them in numerical order.

Obviously, spring is going to feel like liberation.

I always save a few particularly difficult cases for the winter – aberrant specimens of critical families with many species: *Platycheirus, Cheilosia, Sphaerophoria*. Insects whose names arouse uncertainty as well as hopes of some small advance at the outermost limits of human knowledge. Restful handiwork, and exciting. Then – in winter, by air, around the world, on pins, in little aluminium film cans padded with bubble wrap – the most peculiar of these flies travel to renowned and respected experts of oracular status in service of the art of decoding the meandering choreography of the German classification tables.

A sea eagle, broad as a banner at a protest march, streaks past over the ice outside my window, and sometimes the crossbills are busy out there in the dusk dropping cones on the terrace from the spruce at the corner, which I vow to cut down every autumn for the sake of the light. Ravens reconnoitre from the top of the telecom mast on the other side of the village whose age no one knows. Otherwise nothing. The north wind and the west wind and half-smothered rumours of the villagers' indiscretions and despair. When spring finally arrives in March, my flies sit in neat, straight rows, except for a few that endlessly travel or have been caught somewhere like nameless foot soldiers in the ranks of biology's army of inadequately identified fly families. An empty space in the drawer is also a discovery.

In March, I begin sitting in the sun on the steps, and it is then, long before the snow is gone, before the woodlark, the robin and the joggers, that the first flies appear, although not hoverflies but attic flies, so called because they spend the winter in attics. They belong to the blowfly family, interesting creatures themselves, but not a fly one collects from sheer childish delight. At least not so far as I know. Unless possibly in March, when the buzz of any fly at all will pass as a hopeful harbinger of summer. There is something unalterably ominous about blowflies – the musty odour of cadavers and William Golding – which makes no one happy, with the possible exception of those inscrutable forensic entomologists who take pride in solving murder cases by studying the larvae of flies and other insects with names like *Sarcophagus*, *Thanatophilus* and *Necrophorus*, found in the victim's viscera. Based on the creatures that live in the dead and on their stage of development, such people can say an astonishing amount about when the crime was committed and, in certain cases, even determine that it did not occur where the body was found but took place somewhere else. A gloomy science with a truly stable market only in the USA. One can learn more about this subject in order to broaden one's scientific knowledge, but its practical utility is generally limited. Moreover you lose your appetite. And all you remember afterwards is the story of the Finnish charlady.

It was towards the end of the 1970s. A government bureaucrat in Finland found a number of fat fly larvae under the rug in his office. He immediately summoned the char. How in the world, he asked her, had his office come to be crawling with maggots? The charlady had no good answer. She might of course have made a number of amusing replies, some quite sarcastic, but she did not. She said only that she didn't know, but that in any case it was not her fault. Where the maggots came from was a mystery. She had taken out the rug and beaten it only the day before, on that point she was absolutely certain. But the bureaucrat did not believe her, and so the charlady was given her notice on the spot. She was found guilty of having cleaned badly. And in addition she had lied. So good riddance.

The incident was much discussed in government circles, however, and very soon a curious veterinarian appeared and asked to have a closer look at the maggots. He could not understand how such healthy fly larvae could have grown fat on the synthetic fibre used at that time in Finnish government rugs, and in hopes of clearing up the mystery he showed the creatures to an entomologist with a taste for forensics, a man who could see at once that these were larvae of the blowfly *Phaenicia sericata*, ready to pupate. This species, the entomologist explained, hatches in various kinds of carcasses, for example dead mice in the walls of a building, and when they have eaten their fill they leave the corpse at night and wander about in search of a suitable place to pupate. This was how the larvae had wound up under the angry bureaucrat's rug. The charwoman was given back her job. It is not known if the Finnish government apologized.

You never know in advance what knowledge may be good for, however useless it may seem. More than 500 species may be involved in the decomposition of a large cadaver.

Of course it's repulsive. I completely agree. But there is something more. Let me relate another anecdote before we return to my graceful and thoroughly delightful hoverflies. For some time now, I have been hearing reports of a study carried out by several entomologists on the mainland which has every prospect of becoming legendary. If nothing else, it will serve as an example of the irrepressible urge of curious boys to explore islands, even where islands don't exist. Or, to be more exact, where islands are not to be discovered without the creative imagination that characterizes artists and good scientists.

Such islands are all to be found in the archipelago of buttonology. We will have cause to return there later. This is only an initial reconnaissance.

As the curtain goes up, someone has accidentally run over a badger, which now lies by the side of the road, dead. A short time later, one of these imaginative entomologists comes driving peacefully down the same road. He sees the badger and stops his car, climbs out, and considers what has happened. The scene is easy to picture. Solitary driver bent over dead badger on an April day. He thinks. He has an idea. He heaves the body into the trunk and drives on.

This will perhaps remind some readers of Hans Christian Andersen's fairy tale 'Clod Hans', about a boy who finds a dead crow on the road and takes it with him, because you never know when a dead bird will come in handy. This is roughly what happened this time too, with the difference that this time the finder knew right away what he could use the carcass for.

(Actually, Clod Hans knew as well. He was going to give it to the princess, which he later did. Her delight at this gift is one of Danish literature's most puzzling passages.)

A year earlier, this particular scientist had taken a great interest in a cat he found squashed by a car 'in the Forest of Brandbergen', as he wrote in an article about the incident and all its consequences, published in the English journal *Entomologist's Gazette*.

It turned out to be worth writing about, for our motorist and his friends began studying how the cadaver's fauna of resident beetles took shape and changed during all the different phases of decomposition. They kept at it for four months. Altogether they captured 881 beetles, divided into no fewer than 130 different species, which is a lot. Similar research projects in other parts of the world haven't even come close.

This got them started. The beetles in the cat (by now completely eaten) raised a number of questions about the behaviour of necrophagous fauna in general and about its dependence on the nature of the substrate on which decomposition takes place. In addition, they felt the experiment was worth expanding for the obvious reason that cadavers are like islands, where colonization and the development of the ecosystem can be followed from the very beginning, roughly the way it was on Surtsey, the volcanic island that rose from the ocean off the coast of Iceland. Or on Krakatoa in the Sunda Strait between Java and Sumatra, which blew up so completely in 1883 that both fauna and flora had to begin again from nil.

A badger was just what they needed, and they placed it in the same area. But in contrast to the cat case, which played out on an ordinary wooded slope with birch trees and flowers and moss on the ground, they now chose a much drier and biologically poorer location, a higher, stony spot where the plant life consisted of nothing but heather and scruffy pines. Here the dead badger had its resting place, and to prevent some fox from dragging it away when no one was looking, they put it inside a steel cage of the kind normally home to half-tamed rabbits and guinea pigs that run on treadmills. This too is easy to picture. Stone-dead badger in narrow pet cage in the woods. The sight was bizarre enough that they felt compelled to put a little sign on the cage explaining that this was a scientific experiment.

I sometimes think I would like to have such a sign myself.

. . .

There is a day in April when the southern sun opens the buds on the earliest sallows, and on that day the first hoverflies appear. Tiny, unprepossessing species that the books often describe as rarities, perhaps because they really are quite rare, but more probably because no one sees them. People collect insects mostly in summer, during the holidays. It has always been so, and for that reason the summer fauna is better known than the flies of early spring, which sometimes fly for only a week or two. Moreover, the best sallows are usually so tall that you can't reach them with your net. You can stand under them with binoculars and watch everything going on in the flowers up top and rack your brains trying to guess which species are flying around up there. Of course you can buy a longer handle for your net (the inventive Czechs market a handle that is eight metres long) and stand there in the spring sun like a pole vaulter lost in the woods, but those long-handled nets are said to be difficult to manoeuvre with your dignity intact, so instead I have found some sallows that are short but still bloom. Four or five bushes, here and there on the island. And there I spend those days in April when the sun shines and the grass grows so fast that the dry leaves rustle on the ground. Which bush I choose depends on the direction of the wind. Then comes the blue hepatica. Followed by the white hepatica, fig buttercups, marsh marigolds, cowslips, and by the time the maples bloom in the middle of May, all the cares of the winter are forgotten.

The colour alone puts me in a good mood. Maple blossoms are greenish yellow, and the tender leaves a yellowish green – and not the other way around. From a distance, the mix of these two tones creates a third so beautiful that the language lacks a word to describe it. As we all know, greenery deepens in colour as summer comes on, but the blooming of the maples is when it all begins, when everything is at its brightest and best. Just a week, maybe two, and then the alders burst into leaf in deadly earnest. I wish so profoundly that everyone knew. 'Maples blossoming'. Those two words on answering machines would be enough. Everyone would get the message. They'd see the colour, sense its nuance, understand. Know that then everything flies, absolutely everything. A thousand commentaries. An entire apparatus of footnotes.

Chapter 6

René Malaise (1892–1978)

René Edmond Malaise was born in Stockholm and was captivated early in life by the siren song of entomology. Always the same pattern. Is there a single one of us anywhere whose debut came later than childhood?

According to family legend, the decisive impulse in his case occurred during a summer holiday in France with a cousin who collected butterflies. He got started himself that same day. He had already mastered botany, for his mother was the daughter of a gardener, or perhaps it came from the fact that a well-filled herbarium was a self-evident piece of baggage for a boy of good family. His father was a star chef, a French immigrant who was for many years the head chef at the Opera Cellar. From him, René inherited a good deal of restaurant know-how, later also some money, but no interest at all in food. On the contrary, all his life he felt that the important thing was nutritive value, not flavour. There were many tales through the years of scurvy and spit-roasted bear.

Malaise was a born hunter and developed early on a taste for unusual prey and extravagant methods. He liked to tell people about his career as a sharpshooter when, at the turn of the century, the family lived in an apartment on one of the upper floors of a building on Östermalm Square. Inspired by some tropical adventure story, he had made himself a blowpipe and practised his aim by shooting plumed darts into the elaborate hats of ladies in the square below.

Butterflies too were only preparation. A few years to learn the trade. If I understand him correctly, he knew that Swedish butterflies had been thoroughly studied years earlier. There wasn't much new to discover, and supplementing earlier achievements was simply not his cup of tea. He wanted to be a pathfinder, to be his own man.

He chose sawflies. His reasons are unclear, but it was probably because no one else was giving them serious study. Not in Sweden. On top of which, no one had ever dealt adequately with the taxonomy of sawflies, or *Tenthredinidae*, as they are known to science. They had the reputation of being generally troublesome creatures and hard to identify, the very sort of animal on which a young man could become an authority without conducting too many time-consuming studies in the field or in uneventful museums. A Linnaean career lay open before him. The adventures which, while they cannot slake, can still partially satisfy the yearnings of an uneasy soul, lay just around the corner.

During his time at the university in the 1910s, consequently, he undertook his first three expeditions, all to the mountains of Lapland. Not especially original, but suitable for a future sawfly expert, and in any case these trips had been journeyman expeditions for natural scientists of every kind for generations. He did not travel alone. Not yet. At this time he was accompanied in Lapland by another young field biologist, bird-watcher Sten Bergman, and for reasons we can only guess at, their fantasies about the future bounced along with all the uncontrollable joy and nuttiness of lemmings. Eager fingers roamed the map of the world while bluethroats sang in the midnight sun. There!

When, in an earlier age, Carl Jonas Love Almqvist wrote *The Significance of Swedish Poverty* in 1838, his own finger came to rest on the same magical spot.

When we observe the map of the globe, we see, farthest up in the northeast corner of the Old World Continent, a peninsula curving southward, embraced by the open sea. This is Kamchatka. It is very solitary, cut off from the civilized world. But Kamchatka has a counterpart. Farthest up in the northwest corner of the same World Continent, we see, at an even more northerly latitude, another large peninsula, which also curves southward, received and cut off by the sea. This is Scandinavia.

Of all European countries, none is so separate and self-dependent as our Nordic peninsula. Literarily and politically, all the other nations are more or less integrated. They support one another like siblings. Our country is virtually an island, and so we are isolated in the geographical sense. But no less an island is our entire turn of mind, which is dependent only on itself. Everything Scandinavian must stand or fall on its own. In various respects it compares well with the rest of Europe in name; *not so well in reality.*

The boys would go to Kamchatka! A scientific expedition that they themselves would lead, for the purpose of comparing these two so very analogous protuberances on the world map, their fauna and flora, their people. Adventure, perhaps fame. Certainly a wealth of hymenoptera.

In the spring of 1919, a third member joined their planned expedition – the gifted botanist and, in the fullness of time, renowned geographical botanist Eric Hultén, born in 1894, the same year as Bergman. Now all they needed was money. And as Bergman had an incomparable gift of the gab, and was a master at luring sponsors out of the woodwork, backers were soon waiting in line. In Bergman's bestseller about the Kamchatka expedition, a book translated into many languages in the 1920s, several pages of the Foreword are devoted to grateful acknowledgements. They won the Vega Scholarship of the Swedish Society for Anthropology and Geography, along with other, similar travel grants, established in memory of men like Lars Johan Hierta (Sweden's first great champion of the freedom of the press) and Johan Wahlberg (the man who died under an elephant), not to mention an astonishingly long list of war-profiteers who positively bathed in money after the war and who seem to have competed for the privilege of contributing cash to what in their eyes was a fine old Swedish national sport with considerable market value.

You have to wonder if the expedition had any expenses at all. They were given everything – clothes, canned goods, weapons, gunpowder, cameras, skis, lamps, tobacco, toothpaste, everything. The Örebro Cracker Company sent them half a ton of crackers,

Marabou 150 kilos of chocolate, and the Sundbyberg Macaroni Factory added enough dry pasta for an army. And the drink! Of course Bergman was the very model of a tiresome teetotaller, so he doesn't say much about it, just mentions that the state spirits monopoly supported science with a generous cask of preservative. On the other hand, Hultén, who, like Malaise, had never really understood the charm of temperance, remembered that detail in particular when, more than fifty years later, he took pen in hand to write his memoirs under the title *But It's Been Fun*.

The most remarkable gift was nevertheless the spirits. Sweden was under the tyranny of a dictatorial system of alcohol rationing invented and closely controlled by a man named Ivan Bratt, and many saw their ration book as an invaluable possession. But Bratt granted us not only a steel barrel of 96 per cent alcohol for preserving specimens but also – believe it or not – a full ration of spirits for every member of the expedition for three years, the only condition being that we not open the crates until the ship had left Gothenburg harbour.

It does sound like the boys had a very good time, but on one point we must nevertheless correct Hultén, for the most remarkable gift was not the strong drink or even one of Bergman's many cunning advertising projects. He may have been peerless at the art of chatting up cracker-makers and the owners of companies like the Norrköping Raincoat Factory, but the most lucrative triumph of all belonged to Malaise, our hero, who, drunk and happy, caught sight of Anders Zorn one evening at Den Gyldene Freden.

Might he possibly consider a donation in support of a scientific expedition to a foreign land?

Yes, indeed. The very next morning, René Malaise visited the world-famous painter in his atelier, where Zorn, a bit hung over, recalled his promise of the evening before and wrote out a cheque for 10,000 crowns. It was a nice round sum, to say the least – roughly twice the annual income of an average Swedish worker – especially when you stop to think that he wanted nothing in return except pictures of naked Japanese girls. Although he never got them. The cheque is dated 20 May 1919, and Zorn had only one more year to live.

Financially, they were now home-free, and I imagine that the three friends felt that rare happiness that can transform the period between the completion of preparations and actual departure into the most pleasant part of a long journey. You never own the world the way you do before you leave.

. . .

When the days are numbered, everything seems clearer, as if the time between preparation and departure possessed a particular magic. The endless stretch of time on the other side always struck me as evasive and treacherous. But the very limited period between now and then held a liberating peace and quiet. This allotment of time was an island. And the island became, later, a measurable moment. For a long time, this discovery was the only truly unclouded dividend that I took from my travels.

. . .

They left in February 1920, six people altogether. Both Bergman and Hultén were newly married; their wives, Dagny and Elise, came along as field assistants and housekeepers. In addition, they had hired a conservator named Hedström, whose job it was to skin and preserve what they hoped would be large collections of mammals, birds, and whatever else came within range of Bergman's rifle. Malaise himself would take care of the insects. He too had had an offer of marriage before their departure, from the very young but already famous journalist Ester Blenda Nordström, but as the arrangement was to have been merely a marriage of convenience, Sten Bergman exercised his veto, as if it had already been decided that it was he and he alone from whom posterity would hear the story of the Kamchatka expedition.

For just that reason, his story has never interested me. I find that Bergman's thick book about their three years of privation does have a certain value, for he was a good observer and very industrious, but it all pales before the fact that he tries so hard to follow in the footsteps of the great explorer Sven Hedin, which he never succeeded in doing. He was born too late, in the wrong age. The expedition gets only as far as Alexandria (and Bergman only to page one of his book) before

> *. . . people of all sorts, both coloured and white,*
> *crowded past one another, most of them clad in a*
> *kind of commodious trouser-skirt, and it was with*
> *the greatest reluctance that we ventured to entrust our*
> *trunks to the Negro chieftains and Arabs of dreadful*
> *countenance who assaulted us, the one filthier and*
> *more ragged than the next.*

Cheap exoticism built on racist vulgarity was of course standard fare at the time, but Bergman went on like that for another fifty years. If only he hadn't taken himself so awfully seriously.

Once they had arrived on the Kamchatka peninsula, after four months at sea, the Swedes installed themselves in the provincial capital, Petropavlovsk, where, rather surprisingly, the theatre in the Hall of the People was presenting Strindberg's *The Father*, which may have softened the impression of having landed at the back of beyond, at least until they learned that the playwright was thought to be a Dutchman called Stenberg. They were far away, even from Moscow. The Revolution itself seemed distant and somehow preliminary. Red

Guards and counter-revolutionaries traded control of the city under more or less tragicomic forms, while a Japanese cruiser lay anchored in the harbour to watch over the interests of the emperor.

Lives were lost in the sporadic skirmishes between Reds and Whites, but the Swedes were at home in both camps and moved freely. The Hulténs went south one summer to botanize, the Bergmans and Hedström headed north to shoot birds and study the natives, and Malaise, well, exactly what he was up to is not always so easy to determine. He himself wrote very little about those years, and in the books of the others he prowls about in the margins. Some of the time he is simply missing, or else he appears unexpectedly, like a cat that's been lost for months. He seems mostly to have operated by himself in the back country. Sten Bergman writes:

Here our paths diverged for a time. Malaise headed off to the village of Maschura, situated 70 versts farther upriver, in a dugout canoe paddled by two Kamchatkans. From there he later started off with

one native and some horses for Kronoki, a large lake
that lies between the Kamchatka River and the sea.

He caught insects, slew bears, photographed volcanoes and drew maps. Mile after mile of uninhabited territory, often unexplored. Alone. It is said that he was always in exceptionally good spirits. But what was he thinking?

And what made him decide to stay? When the expedition had finished its work in the autumn of 1922 and started home by way of Japan, Malaise remained behind. He was the oldest of them, though not yet thirty. Bergman writes:

Despite its tangled mountain forests and swampy
tundra, its blizzards and its cold, Kamchatka had
nevertheless captured our hearts in these years. All
our sufferings and hardships were forgotten, but we
had crystal memories of all our wonderful evenings
around our campfire in the depths of the wilder-
ness with bears as our neighbours, of clear, starry
winter nights among snow-covered mountains and

*volcanoes, and of unforgettable hours in the shadowy
yurts of the nomads.*

*It was hard to tear ourselves away from all this,
and one of our comrades could not. Malaise was so
enchanted by this land that he decided to stay for several more years. Kamchatka has an almost magnetic
attraction for everyone who has learned to know it
well. It is hard to get there, but it is even harder to
leave it behind.*

Malaise was the proof. For another eight years, until
1930, he simply disappeared without a trace for long
periods. No one knew where he was or what he did.
Back home in Stockholm, among his friends in the
Entomological Society, rumours eventually began to
circulate that he was the manager of a Soviet sable
farm. And what about his relationships with women?
Still today, no one can say with certainty how many
times he was married, or why.

Dagny Bergman also wrote a book about her
youthful adventure, in many ways more charming and
with greater immediacy than the book her husband

85

managed (or wanted) to produce, in spite of the fact that she hadn't the time to write it until their children had left home, towards the end of the 1940s. 'For days on end, Malaise's insect net fluttered across bushes and thickets,' she writes in one place, but otherwise he is often missing from her book too, absent on some vague errand. His name hardly comes up. At the same time, it is she, perhaps, more than any of the other friends on the Kamchatka expedition who comes closest to solving the riddle of René Malaise.

One meets people with the strangest fates in Kamchatka, wind-driven people who have fallen out with society and been forced to disappear, unhappy people who have lost their loved ones in revolution and war, people who have managed to hold themselves erect despite trials of every kind.

. . .

'What's your interest in Malaise?'

The question always took me by surprise. My

answer was along the same lines – evasive. I had begun to collect what little is known about René Malaise. Bought his books, poked through archives, though without finding much. All of the older entomologists I'm acquainted with had of course met him, perhaps heard his hair-raising stories from the 20s, but none had known him well. I got nothing but banalities, a picture of a happy gadabout who knew sawflies and invented a trap, a man with an adventurous past who later became an odd duck, an original whom no one took seriously, who made enemies and finally got lost among the legends. What did I want with him?

Every time I thought I was beginning to understand him, he glided away and vanished into some new kind of craziness, and so every time I let him go and turned to other things. Not because I'd stopped wondering about his fate, but more because his fundamentally expansive, uncontrollable temperament made me uneasy. There was something about him that was boundless.

Chapter 7

Narcissiana

The American psychoanalyst Werner Muensterberger has pointed out that many collectors collect to escape the dreadful depressions that constantly pursue them. He takes up the question in his study of the Holy Roman Emperor Rudolf II (1552–1612), one of the greatest of the truly obsessive collectors, and I'm happy to grant his point, at least if we're talking about art or books or other objects that change hands in the marketplace and are more or less difficult to find. People who collect everything, as long as it's curious enough, are especially likely to be engaged in a form of fetishism that does indeed allay anxiety.

I know, for I was once on the verge of buying a house in Ydre solely because a dilapidated outhouse on the property was said to have belonged to the once famous poet and bishop Esaias Tegnér (1782–1846).

Natural objects, on the other hand, are not fetishes in the same way. One reason is that they can seldom be purchased for money. In addition, they almost always lack cultural provenance. Any beetle whatsoever that was caught, pinned and classified by, say, Charles Darwin, would be a wonderful fetish with which to cure a depression, but such things are impossible to come by. It's true that I own a stuffed peacock whose history is known, including a list of everyone who's owned it since it died in the nineteenth century, and any desperate character who came along might buy it. But the normal thing these days is that nature collectors catch the creatures themselves. That's different from dealing in art.

I have a distinct feeling that Freudians in general have a much too diffuse picture of the passions that may express themselves in, say, fly-hunting. They are way too locked into their squalid little standard explanations of human behaviour. Thus the aforementioned Muensterberger comes to the conclusion that your average collector represents an 'anal type' who, if I understand the thing correctly, becomes a collector because in his childhood he was not given sufficient time to play with his excrement. It's breathtaking. Not even my good friend the surrealist poet really fits in that package.

I run into him occasionally at Entomological Society meetings. An odd fellow, certainly, but no worse than the others. I like him a lot, partly because his utterly incomprehensible poems make my own books look like wonders of clarity and logic, partly because in addition to his writings he guards a position as one of northern Europe's most distinguished experts on the range and habits of dung beetles. He was out here on the island a couple of years ago, collecting. Freudians would have gone into ecstasies if they could have seen us strolling through meadows, poking at sheep shit or hunkering down beside a fairly fresh pile of horse manure for a professional assessment. No, these are things they just don't understand.

That I take the trouble to bring up Werner

Muensterberger is because he is not always wrong. On the contrary, I think he finds his way through the mist with frightening accuracy when he writes in his book on the psychology of collecting that one thing most collectors have in common is a fairly pronounced narcissism. Well, what can I say? If nothing else, he deserves our attention for supporting his thesis with a touching little story about one of his most interesting cases, a man who falls into the unusual category of 'one-object collectors'.

This man collects only a single article.

One objection is, of course, that one article cannot very well constitute a collection. But the man is special in the sense that he displays many of the manic collector's tragicomic characteristics. He is constantly in search of a better, finer, single specimen, and when he has found it, he immediately gets rid of the old one. One object, neither more nor less. And what drives him is a compelling, intense desire to be seen and acknowledged for his exquisite taste, his mastery. The object, and vice versa – the narcissistic collector in his most crystalline form.

This is perhaps an option for an art collector with a small flat. But collecting a single fly? I don't think so.

But if you did, it would have to be the narcissus fly, *Merodon equestris*. A highly varied species, somewhat like the Adam-and-Eve among orchids, though with more colours than just two. On top of which it's one of those hoverflies that buzzes in such a distinctive way that you can recognize it with your eyes shut, which produces a particularly restful sense of well-being.

Not that I'm in the habit of wandering around outdoors with a blindfold, but it sometimes happens that I need to rest my over-exerted, fly-spying eyes for a spell and just stare at the clouds, or at nothing, lying on my back in the grass and moss on the granite slopes. And to hear the quite singular buzz of a passing narcissus fly in the course of such a summer nap is a pleasure, for the simple reason that knowledge is pleasing.

I know this stuff. No one knows more about the flies on this island than I do. The mere sound can be like recognizing someone you know in the crowd on a railway platform. A friend who tells a story, as if in passing, about the yearning of people long since dead for beauty, for the fragrance of an evening in late May when the air is still.

As early as the Middle Ages there were people in our country who were happy enough and rich enough to import narcissus bulbs from distant southern lands. *Narcissus poeticus*, the Easter lily, and other bulbous plants in beautiful and ugly colours began then to bloom in garden beds and parks across wide areas of the country, but oddly enough it was only in the 1910s that the narcissus fly arrived. The man who first spotted it, outside Helsingborg, was a still unknown elementary school teacher named Oscar Ringdahl. He told the world about his find with a short notice in *Entomologisk Tidskrift*. The year was 1911. He was twenty-six years old. The rest is history, at least for entomologists.

Oscar Ringdahl became a great man, something of a legend. They called him Fly Ringdahl.

As a youth he began collecting beetles and butterflies and did it with such energy that on one occasion, in pursuit of an attractive beetle, he crawled right under

a bench where a pair of lovers sat kissing. But he
quickly decided that flies were more fun than other
insects, possibly because so little was written about
them. He had only a book from 1866 about the people
and natural history of Finland in which there was
anything about flies. Then he read a work in Latin
by Zetterstedt. With these two antiquated books in
his baggage, he set out on a hunt for flies that lasted
his entire life.

As a brief biography, that's not half bad. The quotation
is taken from a 1944 issue of the weekly magazine *Idun*
and is as good a testament as any to his fame. The article
also mentions his wife, Anna, an obviously understanding woman. '"Oscar gets so excited every spring when
the flies start buzzing. It makes him forget all the aches
and pains of winter," says Mrs Ringdahl, and her husband laughs.' By that time (he had a long life) his collection already contained 60,000 flies.

The larvae of the narcissus fly live in the bulb
itself, underground, and they probably established
themselves in Sweden by stealing a ride in bulbs being

sent from Holland. No one knows for sure, of course, but my guess is that's how it happened. One clue is that the famous fly expert George Henry Verrall writes in his 1901 book about the hoverflies of the British Isles how, on 8 June 1869, he caught the very first English specimens of this fly in his brother's garden on Denmark Hill in south London, which received annual shipments of Dutch narcissus bulbs.

The narcissus fly is now common both in England and here in Sweden, even though the various species of the genus *Merodon* are native to the warmer climate of the Mediterranean. Or were. Now they're native here too. This fly may have come as an immigrant from the south a long time ago, but now it has the same residency rights as any other fly. This is my basic political position. Not a very risky one, I have to admit, but that's only because fly politics have never really caught on. Why, I don't know. Spanish snails, mink, wild boar, cormorants, what have you – they all attract a steady stream of populist xenophobes and loudmouths of every kind, but no one cares about flies. Not even the paranoids keep me company. But it is political. And in fly questions I am a liberal and do not insist on a closely regulated transition period before they can be incorporated into our fauna. Let them come. We've got plenty of room.

The question of alien species is quite complex and sensitive. I don't intend to go into it deeply. But I would like to note that the hoverfly hunter can hardly be anything but tolerant in the matter of alien species because he spends his time in the border country, literally, between culture and nature, in a microworld governed by constant coincidence and incessant disturbance. Everything is changing, all the time. I am drawn to gardens – and to meadows, the few that are left. For me, they are wilder and richer and much more fun than nature undisturbed by human beings. And so are pastures, avenues, churchyards, roadside ditches and, in the woods, the abruptly clear-cut galleries for power lines. That's where you find flies! Untouched nature has its merits, certainly, but it rarely measures up to lands that people have disturbed.

Almost any disturbance at all can create a whole new environment, which may sometimes meet the rather intricate demands that some insignificant fly makes on life. It can be quite simple. Let's say that a young landscape architect falls in love with a girl who says she adores the heavy fragrance of balsam poplar, whereupon he, of course, has an entire forest of balsam poplar planted, perhaps at a university that hires him to design its landscaping just at the time he's falling in love, and at night these woods come to be used as a meeting place by, say, the semi-secret Students for the Liberation of White Russia, who put up completely unreadable posters about their hopeless struggle on the smooth trunks of the fast-growing poplars, using the only tool their organization has a plentiful supply of, namely White Russian thumbtacks, which contain indeterminable metallic impurities that give rise to a rare form of rot in the tree's inner bark that some even rarer hoverfly's sap-eating larvae require in order to survive to adulthood.

Even more wondrous is how these flies find the trees to begin with. I suspect that they have spies out circulating everywhere.

I particularly want to emphasize the importance

of love in this context. All too often, love is the unappreciated factor in the development of the culturally determined ecosystems that today harbour the richest menageries of hoverflies. Historically, it was probably the privations of poverty that led people to shape the landscape in ways favourable to flies, but today that landscape is shaped more by wealth and desire. Gardens are the best example. Now that there are no more farmers on the island, it is in gardens we find the greatest wealth of fauna.

. . .

I don't know if the Russians brought any new plants or animals when they laid waste to the island and burned the houses in 1719, but suspicion of strangers from the east has never completely lost its grip on the residents. The fact that a one-year-old great cormorant caught in a fisherman's net had been banded in Murmansk did nothing to improve the cormorant's already dubious reputation, and if more people knew what the narcissus fly's offspring were so diligently up to in the guts of the flower bulbs, I can imagine that it too would incur the wrath of gardeners and provoke clumsy attempts at eradication.

On the other hand, no one has touched the oddity at Silver Lake. Even though it comes from the New World.

It was one of my first years out here, at a time when, like the man who loved islands, I was devoting my summers to compiling a catalogue of all the island's plants. One day I walked out to Silver Lake to have another look at it and to smell the smells I'd smelled before. The lake itself is a bottomless pool, as black as the lakes in John Bauer's wash drawings, and it lies in the midst of a quagmire in the middle of the island in the deepest woods, where people have never lived. There are eight other lakes on my island, all of them larger, their shores lined with cottages, flagpoles and peeling rowing boats asleep among the alder saplings, reeds and loosestrife. Only Silver Lake lies off the beaten track. And nothing is more stable than a quagmire.

How hard it is to find the place, and then find your way home again, is something even Strindberg had to learn. He borrowed the name of the lake for a bitter short story about his loneliness and distress after his divorce from Siri von Essen. She and the children were with him on the island that first summer, then never again. His protagonist, a museum curator, sets out for the lake to fish but gets lost, and although he is an enlightened man who carries the natural sciences like a cast-iron defence against the dark powers, he soon finds himself entangled in a formless struggle with capricious malevolence. 'He recognizes every sound and knows every plant and animal, so if he heard or saw anything strange, he would consider it impermissible.'

I wonder what would have happened if he'd caught sight of what I saw in the sucking peat moss right at the edge of the lake. An American purple pitcher plant. For a moment, nothing was heard but the rustle of a dragonfly's wings.

An alien, carnivorous plant, several feet tall, as imposing as if it had come straight from John Wyndham's classic thriller *The Day of the Triffids*. Just one lonely, magnificent plant. How it got there no one knows, and I can assure you that there's no truth to the rumour, widespread among botanists, that I put it there myself.

It's true that it could have been me, but it wasn't. Which hasn't kept me from entertaining very warm feelings for the purple pitcher ever since that day, not because it catches flies in its fluid-filled leaf cups, or because it's so rare, but rather because, in the manner of naturalized intruders, it breaks a pattern and astounds. Biological xenophobia is widespread but almost always unwarranted.

A little havoc, if only in the form of a garden, seldom does any harm. It goes awry only when the scale gets too large. That was one of the few things that travel taught me.

. . .

Tropical rain forest is at its best on television. Of course it sometimes happens that the jungle is both beautiful and enjoyable in real life, up close, but believe me, it is more often a kind of disgusting orgy where everything pierces and bites and your clothes stick to your body like cling film. You see nothing of the sun because rank foliage arches over the trail like a musty cellar ceiling and torrential rains turn the path to a slippery drainage ditch where only blood-sucking leaches can get a foothold. You are attacked by malaria-infected mosquitoes, and the mere thought of snakebite and broken bones and dysentery sinks your spirits like a stone, since the distance to the nearest road begins to be measured in days, as is often the case in the tropics. Visitors from northern lands, initially so headstrong and adventurous, stand in the dusk on the sodden, rotting floor of the rain forest, downhearted, drained, and speak of nothing but the consistency of their excrement and, beyond that, manage to think only very short thoughts. Get me out of here. Get me a beer.

But you couldn't write about that, not in the early 80s when all the miseries between the Tropics of Cancer and Capricorn were measured, ridiculously, in units of football-fields-clear-cut-per-second. And if I nevertheless ventured to say something to the effect that Central Africa might benefit from some motor-ways and pulp mills, people dismissed it as my way of being provocative, which it was not, or else they said that I was just trying to get attention, which wasn't true either, except maybe a little.

Narcissus poeticus spreads its fragrance in the spring evening. Narcissus flies sing in the undergrowth like tuning forks. The high-frequency hum of their wings is like a footnote that makes the experience all the richer for those who know the sound.

. . .

The last thing I needed was a house in Ydre, especially not in Svinhult, but that's where it was, walking distance from nowhere in Småland.

I saw the ad by chance. Late seventeenth-century log-house in need of renovation. The lot was large and the price so ridiculously low that my imagination, which needed somewhere to live that day, occupied the place from the moment I saw the ad and sank in its jaws just long enough for curiosity to begin morphing into a desire to possess. The house was really cheap. If it had been on the island, the price would have been twenty times higher, at least. I called the broker, in Tranås, but he knew very little and explained that at that price he wasn't interested in doing much more than running the ad. He referred all questions to the seller.

This proved to be an old gentleman, slightly confused, who lived somewhere out in the woods. He chatted with me long and well, clearly both pleased and surprised that someone had an interest in his hovel. I listened, guardedly, moderately eager to own this ruin at the end of beyond. Troubles you can have for nothing, I thought. Why buy more of them in Svinhult? It was then he said the thing about the outhouse – parenthetically, no big deal, a curiosity perhaps, nothing more. It had belonged to Esaias Tegnér. Then he said that, shortly after Tegnér's death in 1846, an auction was held at Östrabo in Växjö to sell the contents of his house. Even the outhouse was auctioned. For many years it had stood behind the parsonage in Svinhult. Now it was his.

Municipal offices in Ydre confirmed the story. The cabin was old, ramshackle, and there was folklore about the outhouse. I was now bewitched. I called Professor Bergh in Lund, chairman of the Tegnér Society, and he couldn't get a word in edgewise as I poured out my questions about the property auction. He hummed and hawed for a while in confusion, then gave me an experienced assessment of my chances of establishing a provenance for the rotting outhouse. They were small. He himself had never heard of the object, but there was another individual in the society I might speak to. She was an archivist of the old school. If there was anything at all about the outhouse in writing, she would find it if anyone could. I called her. Heard how she slowly shook her head. My pulse resumed its normal rhythm.

Three days later she called me back. It sounded as if she had run to the phone, for she was a little out of breath when she asked me if the outhouse in Svinhult was a two-seater.

'A two-seater it is,' I said.

'There was a two-seater sold after Tegnér died,' she said.

There was bidding on the house, and I hung in there a good bit beyond the starting price. The broker was in Tranås with a telephone in each hand. On the one, me, on the other a bidder from Mariannelund. He got the place for 73,000 crowns. I've never had any regrets. But it was only afterwards that I asked myself what I actually wanted with that house. About the point of the whole thing. The only answer I could come up with was that I had been carried away on a wave of irresistible desire to collect that outhouse. Like a fetish.

'Hi, everyone, I've travelled around the world and I own Tegnér's crapper.'

No, it wouldn't do. Flies are better. They allay anxiety in a different way. On top of which they're free.

Chapter 8

The Riddle of Doros

I have made one exception, only one, from my rigid rule about collecting only on the island. One of the 202 fly species in the rows in my cabinet is a borderline case. It was the satellite man who brought it. *Eristalis oestracea*, the big shaggy one.

A pretty fly, capricious in its behaviour. Perhaps it's had a hard time surviving, because its business plan since immemorial times, maybe millions of years, has been, like a sheep in wolf's clothing, to plagiarize the troublesome gadfly (*Oestrus ovis*). They are truly very similar. A cow can hardly tell the difference, and neither can anyone else. The problem is just that the gadfly was eradicated from this part of the world a long time ago. And so the protective similarity vanished. For this same reason, we stand in open-mouthed wonder at other insects so bizarrely designed that not even a surrealist on drugs could have made them up. Perhaps they are merely imitating something that no longer exists.

Explaining rarity is an art, plain and simple. Sometimes you can't escape the questions of casual observers unless you retell the story of the rare Himalayan dung beetle that once thrived far and wide on the majestic droppings of the woolly mammoth but that now, like a Russian prince in exile, gets along on the meagre manure of the yak. The more I think about it, the more it seems to me it was a great mistake to replace 'natural history' with the uninspired term 'biology'.

But back to the satellite man.

It was the children who christened him. A journalist. A radio announcer of that heroic sort who, early every Saturday morning, year round, tries to create broadcast entertainment by sticking a microphone under the nose of someone who *sees* something – a bird or something. 'Look there! A flock of widgeons!' What can you say?

No one yet has tried to broadcast ballet on the radio, but is this any better? Oddly enough, it often seems to work – more or less – at least to judge by listener polls, but of course refreshing the repertoire is a constant challenge. The bird-watching shelter these people have not visited does not exist. Again and again they stand in these places in the morning mist and chat inanely about the birds they saw last year. They're clearly desperate. So desperate that this summer they've hit on the sick idea of doing some hoverfly radio.

'My, my, look here, we've actually found a little hoverfly. Oops, there it went.'

He arrived the evening before to set up his satellite dish on the lawn, a big parabola, because the whole spectacle was to be broadcast live. But the first thing he did was present me with a small gift, which was droning dully inside the little yellow knit sock they pull over the microphone to cut off the rustling of the wind.

'It was the only thing handy to catch it in,' he said.

A fly. The satellite man had brought a living hoverfly. Instead of candy or a bottle of wine. It had been trying to escape through a closed window on the boat from the mainland, and the announcer thought it was pretty and would make a nice present. I peered cautiously into the sock and closed it up again quickly. Was it really possible? *Eristalis oestracea*. A species I had never seen. Neither before nor since. It became the only exception to my rule.

The radio programme was more run-of-the-mill, not exactly legendary, but years later you could still hear hardened islanders telling each other about the idiot who ran around on the boat trying to catch a bumblebee in a shag sock.

. . .

The boat to the island takes only ten minutes, but the water is very deep. Ten minutes isn't long, but it's enough for a conversation about essential things – land sales, infidelities, maybe a rare-bird sighting. Conversations of this kind on the boat can be very rewarding and pleasant, although the words said are banal and few. They are nevertheless full of vitality, because the journey's duration is measured. Everyone knows how long it will last and they plan what they will say accordingly.

Nothing promotes concentration like a known limitation of time, sometimes of space as well. If you don't know where the limit lies, then it's chatter as usual. Like life itself. Vague and dawdling. Or like one of those conversations that arise when trains are delayed. The train suddenly stops. No one knows why. Time passes. You begin talking to the person sitting beside you, but since neither one of you knows how long the delay will last, the conversation takes no fixed shape. Only when the train starts again and you know how much time you've got, only then do you make real contact. Often right before one of you gets off, or both.

'When are you going home?'

That was always the first question the children asked when people came to visit. Only then were they willing to make acquaintance.

. . .

The genus *Eristalis* consists entirely of impostors, a good dozen species on the island, of which most look like bees. One of the most common – *Eristalis tenax*

– looks so very much like a honeybee that you can seldom be really certain as it whizzes past. Its disguise is so superb that the bluff made its way right into the Bible. No other hoverfly has managed that. At least not as far as I know. The question has never had a high priority among biblical scholars.

The relevant passage is in the fourteenth chapter of the Book of Judges, in the age-old story of Samson, who eventually made the mistake of falling in love with Delilah. Though this was before that, early in the story, when he was on his way to Timnah, near the Arabian Gulf, to court a different woman entirely. As some readers may remember, he is attacked on his way by a roaring lion, which he resolutely and skilfully rips to pieces with his bare hands, for Samson was the Old Testament sort of man who had God at his back and could therefore comfortably slay a thousand Philistines before lunch. Under the circumstances, it's hardly surprising that lions were eradicated in the Middle East. What's remarkable is that the last of them survived into the twentieth century.

In any case, the courtship succeeded and some time

later, when Samson was on his way to the wedding, he once again passed the place where he had killed his lion. Curious, he inspected the remains and found to his amazement that a swarm of bees had taken up residence in the cadaver. Without hesitating, he gulped down some of the honey and then came up with the brilliant idea of putting one over on his wedding guests with a riddle. '"Let me tell you a riddle," Samson said to them. "If you can give me the answer within the seven days of the feast, I will give you thirty linen garments and thirty sets of clothes. If you can't tell me the answer, you must give me thirty linen garments and thirty sets of clothes."'

Hard to imagine what he wanted with all the clothing. Games and gambling were maybe just a way of passing the time during such a long party. In any event, the guests took the bet and asked in unison to hear it. It went like this: 'Out of the eater, something to eat; out of the strong, something sweet.' And of course they couldn't guess it. Not a glimmer.

The only way for the guests to come up with the somewhat far-fetched answer (rotting lion generates bees) was to turn to Samson's new bride and threaten her with arson and death unless she could slyly inveigle a hint from her husband. She did, the guests solved the riddle, and the whole thing ends with the traditional orgy of violence when Samson slays thirty men (which was God's plan from the beginning) before returning home alone, seething with wrath. The rest of the story is all vengeance in various forms until Delilah comes into the picture and everything goes straight to hell. There's not much more to be said. The Book of Judges is like that. What's interesting are the bees.

Those who know the Bible are said to be pretty much in agreement these days that the swarm of bees in the lion's carcass is only an expression of the ancient superstition that honeybees could generate spontaneously from ordure and various kinds of putrefaction. This belief was not questioned until the seventeenth century, and even much later, many people were unwilling to accept the idea that these bees, crawling from the stinking stew of corruption, were nothing but so-called drone flies, *Eristalis tenax*, hoverflies disguised as bees. It was these drone flies that Samson saw. The honey is only one more in a long line of tedious later additions.

. . .

But in the long run, doesn't it get monotonous? Sooner or later, I always get that question. True, the island isn't large. And the number of hoverfly species is not unlimited. Pretty soon they're all there in the drawers. My good friend, the foremost expert, often says that if I'm lucky and live a long time I may find as many as 240 species on the island, hardly more. And years will pass between the last finds. That's just the way the fauna and the island are. Even now, after seven years, I find it hard to catch anything new. But monotonous? No, no. Lonely maybe.

For an entomologist, fifteen square kilometres is a whole world, a planet of its own. Not like a fairy tale you read to the kids again and again until they know it by heart. Nor like a universe or a microcosm, similes I'm not willing to accept, but like a planet, neither more nor less – but with many white patches. Even if I were to swing my net an entire summer without adding a single species to my collection, the gaps in our knowledge will still be great, if not quite immeasurable. The fact is, they keep growing, keeping pace with our knowledge. Like that morning when the world changed.

It was a perfectly ordinary day in July, and I had just seated myself in the morning sun to eat my breakfast and watch the Caspian terns fly in from the outer islands to fish in the lake. At first I noticed nothing unusual, because you always get a little thick-witted along towards high summer, but however that was I glanced out at my oregano patch, which I planted only because the oregano blossoms attract a lot of flies. Something wasn't right, something about drone flies.

It's important to the story to know that I had devoted a lot of time that year to the different species in the *Eristalis* family. They're hard. Well, not *oestracea*, of course, but many of the others. Several very common species look roughly alike, and to tell them apart on pins, you have to sit at the microscope for a long time and vacillate. Sometimes it's easier to identify them in the field, without even catching them, because at least a couple of the drone flies that look very much alike behave quite differently. They fly at different times of the day and they don't visit the same flowers. I'd been amusing myself with these very problems, without making much progress, I have to admit, but I had learned enough to see when something didn't make sense. The flies on the oregano looked to be some completely new species. And even stranger, they were everywhere.

I still find new species every summer, single specimens, unexpected finds, flies that have been here the whole time in such infinitesimal numbers that they've eluded me. I am convinced that no matter how long I continue, my collection will always include some puzzling solitaries. But this was something else. It was, to be sure, a new species – *Eristalis similis* – but the mystery was that my oregano was crawling with them. Just this first day I'm sure I saw hundreds. And they were big, like bees. The scope of the enigma was in the books, where it said that this species had been captured in Sweden only once before, on the island of Gotska Sandön, and only one specimen.

The world had definitely changed. This was an invasion.

It is at such moments that the entomologist becomes a story-teller. He is prepared to do almost anything to get someone to listen and perhaps understand. He is prepared to use any ruse or artifice to avoid being the only one who sees. He can endure solitude better than most, but not at such a moment.

Later I learned that the invasion of *Eristalis similis* had occurred on a broad front all across the country. The species had poured in from the southeast like a cloud, and considering how many I saw on the island that first day, there must have been hundreds of thousands, maybe millions of flies involved. They do that some-times, hoverflies – have a fit and fly away en masse. We don't always know why, but we must assume that this behaviour has its benefits. This particular species seems to have established itself, at least here on the island, for I now see several every year. Of course they too could be migrants, but my guess is that they live here and like the place. In any case, the species that move every year do flourish, the notorious long-distance fliers in families like *Eupeodes*, *Scaeva* and *Syrphus*. Their larvae live on aphids that occur very unevenly, with sudden massive numbers in some particular place, so it pays the flies to operate across large areas. If there are lots of aphids for the moment in some other part of Europe, they fly there. It is completely pointless to band them, unfortunately, and not even the Japanese have managed to build a radio transmitter of an appropriate size, but it is nevertheless possible to map the movements of the most peripatetic hoverflies by examining the grains of pollen in their coats and determining where these originated. It's nit-picking work, but it produces results.

When the rewards of hunting for new species begin to dwindle, I'll probably switch to solving mysteries. There are a lot of them, believe me. Certain species are primarily known for being enigmatic. And one of the biggest of these is *Doros*.

I sometimes hear rumours that the riddle has been solved, that someone has found the larvae and managed to elucidate an intricate relationship with some kind of subterranean aphid that lives in roots, but there is not yet any credible evidence. The case is complicated by the fact that *Doros profuges* is so desperately capricious in its behaviour. Despite being large and attractive and unlike any other insect, and despite its occurrence in almost every European country, we still know almost nothing about it. No one knows what it lives on or why it's so sporadic. It just appears somewhere, a single specimen, and is then not seen again. It is uncommon everywhere. For anyone to find two in the same place is very unusual. Why?

Well, I certainly don't know. But since I have captured seven of them on the island, which is a unique record in Europe, I have my theories. Let's say that the larvae are subterranean and sensitive to the composition of the soil. As mentioned earlier, there are indications that this is the case. Maybe it likes limy soils. That would explain its rarity. Its erratic appearance might then be the result of a maturation that takes several years, which would mean that the fly doesn't fly every year. Of my seven specimens, four are from one year and three from another. Otherwise I haven't seen a trace of them. That could be one piece of the puzzle. Another possible explanation is that *Doros* flies for only a day or two and then dies, like a mayfly. The collector who sees one is just lucky. Only the man who never moves from his spot sees seven. Is there something sad about that fact?

Chapter 9

In the Shadow of a Volcano

On the night between 2 and 3 February 1923, all hell broke loose. The experience stayed with him. Indeed, it became one of the smash hits in his story-telling career, and, over the years, one of the foundations of his ideas about a fairy-tale island that sank in the sea. Or maybe an entire continent. That the ground he stood on was shaky – even his detractors agreed on that. And there came to be quite a few of them.

That winter, Malaise camped in the wilderness with two threadbare Russian fur hunters. They were living somewhere inland from Olga Bay in eastern Kamchatka, hundreds of kilometres from any settlement. Exactly what he was doing there, and on assignment from whom, is, as always, a little unclear, open to speculation, but the official purpose was in any case to continue collecting zoological specimens on behalf of the Swedish Museum of Natural History, and at the same time to do the groundwork for a never completed mapping of the area by taking a long series of panoramic photographs from the tops of mountains. They lived in tents or in indescribably filthy huts of turf and birch logs. Not together, each separately, miles apart – so as not to disturb each other's hunting, they said. A double-barrelled shotgun and a Winchester, a sack of flour, salt, some sable shears. A camera, pots and pans, and high spirits.

It began well. The blizzards were dreadful and the days were short, but after only a couple of months they could change their long underwear because they had found hot springs in a valley between two volcanoes. Their way of life was extreme in its simplicity. They ate meat, boiled or grilled. Wild reindeer, bear, birds. They baked bread in a way that only a bachelor in the woods could have dreamed up. 'In order to avoid carrying or having to make a kneading trough, hunters bake by digging a hole in the flour in the sack, pouring in salt, water, and sometimes baking powder too, then mixing it into dough with a stick, whereupon the flour is removed from the sides of the "trough".' This lump of dough was then boiled in bear fat. Nutrition, nothing more.

Early in February, Malaise went down to the coast alone to fetch supplies and store specimen collections in a storehouse they had there, a few hundred metres from the shore. New snow had fallen during the night, and the trip home was harder than expected. His dogsled was heavily laden, and the surface of the trail was terrible. He had no choice but to spend the night in an old hunter's hut along the way, a dilapidated yurt, its roof beam sway-backed like a hammock beneath the heavy turf roof. He prepared his meagre evening meal on the hut's stove and rolled out his sleeping bag in the dark. Fell asleep at once. Woke up as if he were at sea.

There was a powerful earthquake in Kamchatka that night. He tells the story in his first book, *Hunts and*

Earthquakes. How he just barely managed to crawl out of the yurt before the roof fell in, the terrible roaring noise, the way the birches swayed and threw themselves about in the windless night. He writes about the uncertainty in the grey light of dawn, and how he eventually found his comrades, unhurt but scared to death. On the other hand, their cache on the coast, their boat, even the forests that grew down along the shore had vanished. A tremendous tsunami had driven a wall of ice several kilometres inland like a plough or a carpenter's plane. Everything was gone. And the aftershocks continued. 'For the first three days, the earth shook about every five minutes, later every quarter of an hour, after a month once an hour, and when I left the area at the beginning of July there were one to three earthquakes a day.'

The Russians left a month later. They didn't dare stay, so fearful were they that the land would sink into the sea. They headed south on foot, towards Petropavlovsk, but Malaise stayed on, brazen in his loneliness, actually pleased because the remaining flour would now last longer. Wolves took his dogs, unfortunately, but he seems nevertheless to have kept up his courage until relief arrived. There is a long and sensual passage in his book about the art of preparing pit-roasted bear. 'The fat connective tissue under the bear's feet, which to begin with could compete with gutta-percha for toughness, was now so tender I could eat it with a teaspoon.' Homesickness was not in his vocabulary.

As autumn approached, he went to Japan to buy film. His glass plates had been lost in the tidal wave, and ordering new ones from Kamchatka was easier said than done in the revolutionary confusion. Anyway, there were other things he needed as well. So he got a ride on a boat to Yokohama. Was going to be gone only a few weeks. As usual, things didn't work out the way he expected.

On 31 August 1923 there occurred the largest earthquake in Japan's history – typically, only a few days after our friend Malaise arrived. At the moment of the catastrophe, he was on the second floor of a hotel in Kamakura outside Tokyo, where he had gone with some friends for what was to have been a beach holiday.

He was on his way out of the door when the quake began. 'I had just been telling myself that it was foolish to come to one of Japan's finest beach resorts only to lie around in bed, and that it would be better to go down to the water and see if the breakers rolling in were suitable for what they call surfing.'

I have a hard time picturing René Malaise in bathing trunks with a surfboard under his arm, and that isn't the way it turned out either, for a second later both roof and floor disappeared and the only thing left was Malaise standing in the doorway. 'The building was thrown back and forth like a ship in the most terrible storm.' Quick as a flash he ran for the street, exactly how is unclear since the floor was gone.

Halfway out, a door suddenly opened ahead of me and an elderly, corpulent woman came through it as if shot from a cannon and was thrown against the opposite wall, where she collapsed like a rag. A couple of leaps and I was past her and out to the stairs, but when I turned around and saw her lying there, I was ashamed of myself and went back. I managed to help

her out to the stairs as well and on down to the street.
That the old woman and I were not shaken off the
steps is more than I can explain.

What follows is an incomparable description of the devastation in Yokohama and Tokyo, incomparable because he relates it like a journey through hell – and yet not. A hundred thousand people died in the catastrophe, and Malaise found himself in the middle of the firestorm, saw it all with his own eyes – heaps of bodies, looting – and still he insists on narrating these scenes in the manner of a newsreel, without the slightest concession to his own terror and despair. As if nothing could upset his good spirits. 'There we slept peacefully the whole night, undisturbed by the stronger and weaker aftershocks that shook the ground, while the heavens glowed blood red from Tokyo in flames.'

One possible explanation for this exhilarated style is that he saw a good deal of the Swedish humourist Albert Engström in Moscow on his way home. There was of course no real point in returning to Kamchatka now that all the film in Japan had gone up in smoke.

Anyway, he had missed the last boat of the year. So, homeward. Via Vladivostok. Which was not the easiest trip to make, as his passport lacked the proper visas and permits. But he managed nevertheless, probably because no Soviet border guard in the world could resist this stubborn Swede, who, on top of everything else, had become an official courier, no mean trick under the circumstances. Before he left, a former Russian consul in some Japanese city had given him letters to deliver to a commissar in Vladivostok. For as long as the Soviet Union lasted, this was one of the best ways to clear a path through the bureaucracy.

. . .

It is many years ago now. I had business in Karakalpakia in Uzbekistan and took the 1.35 flight from Stockholm. On the plane, which flies over my island every day at twenty minutes to two, I wound up sitting next to the Moscow correspondent for the evening tabloid *Expressen*. We immediately began bragging to each other.

I was on my way to the Aral Sea. Not so awfully

enviable, perhaps, but worth bragging about, since this happened before the collapse of the empire, and in those days no one went wherever he wanted to go in the USSR. But he was not impressed. He countered instead with a whole series of more or less hair-raising exploits of the kind that all foreign correspondents can tell if pressed. I tried my adventures in northern Siberia the year before. No reaction. His stories began to be absolutely surrealistic.

Short pause. We unbuckled our seat belts.

I waved my letter to the Soviet Minister of the Environment from the Swedish one, Birgitta Dahl, which in a roundabout way had been entrusted to me to deliver personally because the postal service was undependable. The foreign correspondent gave me a look that suggested he had any number of more important documents in his own diplomatic bag. After about fifteen minutes, I had only one more ace up my sleeve.

'Oh, look, this is where I live,' I said, as if in passing, as the island spread out beneath us. It worked. At least a little. If you live in the Stockholm archipelago, you are presumed to earn a great deal of money or at the very least to be some kind of memorable eccentric, and that sort of thing impresses journalists. In fact, few things impress them more. I held my breath and gazed down at the island. Would this impress him? Seconds passed, half a minute, not more. And then, thank goodness, I saw the signal for my decisive thrust.

'You see down there?' I said. 'There, in the middle of the island, on this side of the lake, that flashing light?'

I had the window seat, and the correspondent leaned across me to look down.

Yes, of course, he saw something twinkling on the shore of the lake, whereupon, with the globetrotter's casual ease, I could end the conversation with the words: 'It's a signal. My son, you know, sending us a signal. With the bathroom mirror.'

I was so proud of him for pulling it off. Suddenly my whole hot-air contest with the correspondent struck me as ridiculous and I just leaned back in my seat and smiled.

My seatmate didn't know what to say, just gave

me a grudgingly respectful glance, and before we reached Gotska Sandön, he'd gone off to try to impress someone else.

. . .

Malaise's movements are fairly easy to follow to this point, November 1923. He had been abroad for four years. Now he was back home in Stockholm. And then he goes off the radar.

He wrote his book, which was published the following year, and nothing would have been easier than for him to travel around the country and enjoy his celebrity, the way Sten Bergman had done. As a lecturer. He was good at that. But that isn't what he did. Instead, he went back. In the summer of 1924, he returned to his bleak outpost on the Pacific Ocean. Why?

Two clues: first, there are certain indications that Sten and René had some kind of agreement that Bergman would do all the public relations. I don't know this for a fact, but the family has suggested that, as an old man, Malaise was not altogether happy about having had to play second fiddle. He begins the foreword to his book with an assurance that it is *not* an official description of his participation in the Kamchatka expedition but deals only with the year when he remained behind. As if he were not permitted to write about the first three years. And by the time Malaise returned to Stockholm, Bergman had already become a megastar and secured his place in history.

Did Malaise return to the wilderness to prove something?

Was he fleeing?

Or was he simply in love?

The second clue is that he dedicates the book to an exceptionally dazzling woman – Ester Blenda Nordström. The woman who had not been allowed to go on the expedition in the first place, the woman Bergman had rejected. Perhaps she is the reason René came home and turned right around. I simply can't imagine that it was hymenoptera that lured him away again, and yet I'm one of those who can believe pretty much anything of an entomologist. Whatever the role of the hymenoptera, about one year later Ester Blenda went to Kamchatka as well, and two years to the day after the Japanese earthquake, on 31 August 1925, the two were married.

As I said, the trail grows indistinct at this point, but this much is clear: Malaise remained in the Far East until 1930, and Ester Blenda stayed for two years. I have found one single letter from that time, written by Malaise in December 1927 and addressed to one of his aunts. At the time, he was running a Soviet sable farm in the village of Yelisovo, near Petropavlosk – '250 rubles a month and I don't really have to do anything but walk around, play boss, and point out what needs to be done'. The letter also reveals that, earlier, he had lived with Ester Blenda in another village, Klyuchi, not far from the preposterously beautiful Klyuchevskaya Sopka, Eurasia's tallest active volcano. They had apparently supported themselves as photographers. Now she was gone. He writes, 'You mustn't believe that Ester Blenda and I parted on bad terms, on the contrary, and I am quite certain that she will return.'

She didn't. Their divorce was final in 1929, and

there is no record of any further contact between them. Experts on the Nordström family maintain that their relationship was a marriage in name only. That she was not even interested in men. Others say that she was exploiting a credulous childhood friend. That may be, but equally likely is that they were just two very lonely people in exile who kept each other company where the world is at its most beautiful and most cruel and again most beautiful. But that Malaise, at least, was in love is no wild guess. Everyone loved Ester Blenda. She had something that everyone fell for, both women and men. No one has ever managed to say exactly what, although many have tried.

She was born in 1891 and, still young, made a name for herself in the Stockholm newspapers under the pseudonyms Pojken (The Boy) and, later, Bansai. Her eyes, people still talk about her eyes, their enigmatic charm, so full of contradictions. She was unpredictable, everyone who knew her agrees on that. Socially, she could glitter like a star – an irresistible party girl, high-spirited, funny, inventive, always ready to play a song on her accordion or to tell a good story in the whirl of a giddy evening. But as often as not she was overcome with sadness and withdrew, tore off on her motorcycle or disappeared on long tramps in the wilderness. She travelled a lot, often alone, sometimes incognito. Jack Kerouac had not been born when Ester Blenda Nordström bummed across the United States, hitchhiking, hopping freights and cattle trains.

Her debut as an author was an immediate success. In 1914 she published a book of undercover reporting called *A Maid among Maids* that sold 35,000 copies. Disguised and using a false name, she had taken employment as a housemaid with an unsuspecting farmer in Södermanland. Her book opened up a whole world of social evils whose existence her bourgeois readers had apparently forgotten. The debate was hard and long, and Ester Blenda's name was on everyone's lips. She herself went away to Lapland to work as a nomadic teacher in a Sami village. She was gone for nine months. It was a hard life, but *The People of the Kota* (1916) is one of her best books.

Nowadays, people often compare her with Günter Wallraff, who also was not yet born when she wrote her books, and the comparison is apt. She was just as fearless, just as outrageous, just as drawn to hardship. Even their success is comparable. But there is something this comparison misses. Of course it is her social reporting that people still talk about and that academics still discuss in their genre studies, but it is something else that seduces the reader who picks up one of her books. And this something is a far cry from German hard-hitting journalism.

It's not Wallraff she resembles but, if anyone, Bruce Chatwin. No other Swedish author reminds me more of Chatwin. They are both puzzling, inaccessible and luminous. The same devastating eye and the same unbeatable brilliance in their ability to please. And they were escaping, constantly, perhaps from themselves, leaving behind a trail of dreamy-eyed admirers, questions, and perpetual speculation about disjointed sexuality and conflicting passions of every kind. Even their obsessive interest in nomads and people at the edge of the world, even that is the same, almost identical. Two wanderers who disappeared. What's left is legend. Chatwin died of AIDS at the age of forty-eight. Ester

Blenda Nordström died at fifty-seven after suffering a debilitating stroke at the age of forty-five.

Her most remarkable book, and incomparably her best, is *Village in the Volcano's Shadow* (1930), which is about the years in Kamchatka – 'the golden land of indolence and optimism'. Its epigraph is a line from the poet Robert William Service: 'Lover of the Lone Trail, the Lone Trail waits for you'. It's a funny book, hilarious in places, but at the same time deeply gripping and melancholy. She tells about life in the village – sits at a desk somewhere at home in Sweden and looks back with a sense of loss that carries through all the sometimes uproarious, sometimes tragic human destinies that she describes.

But she never wrote about her husband. Not a line. No doubt he was out somewhere with his net. Yet she is the person who provides the most probable explanation of why René Malaise stayed out there for ten years. I think he was quite simply enjoying himself. It was his kind of landscape.

Klyuchevskaya rages upward towards the sky. It's as if she knows herself to be the world's greatest volcano and therefore longs to reach still higher; as if she were furious at being tied to the earth and broke her way up into space to reach right to heaven in her wild, boundless vanity.

Chapter 10

The Net and Loneliness

Ester Blenda Nordström had an older brother named Frithiof. He was for the most part her exact opposite. Quiet and stationary as a barnacle. A dentist. But he devoted all his free time to collecting butterflies. Over the years, he became the greatest of all experts in Sweden, and his career had its crowning touch from 1935 to 1941 when, with Albert Tullgren, he wrote the magnificent *Svenska fjärilar* (*Swedish Butterflies*), unsurpassed to this day.

He never said much about his mysterious sister. But there is one place in John Landquist's memoirs where Frithiof flits by in an obscure comment about her life.

Professor and literary critic Landquist had been head over heels in love with Ester Blenda years earlier, as, clearly, had his wife at that time, the feminist writer Elin Wägner. Ester Blenda had lived with them for several years in her youth. Landquist writes, 'Years later, after her death, her brother Dr Frithiof Nordström, the famous butterfly expert, told me that she remained strict in erotic matters all her life.' Whatever he may have meant by that.

In any event, it appears that Frithiof Nordström spent several summers here on the island in the 1910s. He collected here and wrote about his finds in *Entomologisk Tidskrift*. Maybe he came here for the butterflies. The island was already known among collectors. The locals were a little crazy, to be sure, but it had a distinctive flora and many unusual insects.

He and I have a social life of the entomological kind. Finding new species that have never before been taken on the island or even in the whole province of Uppland can, of course, be very exciting, but it doesn't compare with finding insects that others saw long ago and that no one has seen since. The ones presumed to have vanished. I cannot describe the feeling other than to liken it to a form of social intercourse, where time means a great deal and nevertheless nothing. If I see a rare butterfly that Frithiof once captured almost a hundred years ago, it's like getting an unexpected picture postcard from an old acquaintance off on a long holiday.

I look forward with impatience to the day when our natural history museums get around to cataloguing their collections in a searchable database the way the Royal Library does in Stockholm. Only then can the postcards get flowing in earnest. As things are, it's impossible to ferret out what other people have caught on the island and when. As soon as a collector at long last dies, the fruits of his life's labours and joys wind up at some museum, usually in Lund or Stockholm, whereupon all of it is amalgamated into the museum's main collection, each species in its own drawer. They do this for practical reasons. And for anyone doing research on a particular insect family, this steadily growing museum collection becomes ever more usable and valuable. At the same time, however, it's like spreading ashes in the wind. Reconstructing a collector's journey is impossible once his prey has been dispersed.

Sten Selander, who also lived out here at that time, described his own collection of stinging wasps as if it were one of his written works. This was in his melancholy essay 'The drawer where summer dwells'. He remembers. They're not pretty, the wasps, not like butterflies . . .

But the hymenoptera have one quality I understand, almost the only comprehensible aspect of these insects' peculiar world – they love sunshine and warmth as intensely as I do. Maybe that's the reason I was drawn to them in the first place. I don't really recall, it's so long ago now. Thanks to this characteristic of the hymenoptera, my collection includes thousands of small labels with the date and place of capture, and these comprise a diary of clear and beautiful days, days of warmth, soft breezes and no other clouds than small, puffy cirri, and above this chest of drawers, where twenty bygone summers sleep, there might

be inscribed the same words written on innumerable
sundials: I count only the happy hours.

He pulls out a drawer at random and begins to read. The sun beats down, a life unfolds. All entomologists sit like this, for as long as they live. Thereafter, their friends.

If there were a database, I would only have to search the collector's name. Or a place. Or both. Now that I've come to know him, it would be nice to know if Malaise was ever out here trapping, for example on a visit to Frithiof one summer. The answer is in his collections, available, unfortunately, only to the person who has time to inspect the tiny labels on several million specimens. Just going through the sawflies would be an insurmountable task. You can get answers to simple questions. Did Frithiof Nordström ever capture *Macroglossum stellatarum* on the island? The hummingbird hawk moth? You can go through that drawer in Lund and learn that the answer is no. And think, 'Too bad, Frithiof. It's flying here now.'

Of course moths and butterflies are nothing to me. Not like flies. They're just something you see all the time and notice involuntarily, almost the way you read newspaper headlines. Like birds, trees and wildflowers, the really big, beautiful moths and butterflies are the introduction to nature's fine print – all the tiny, subtle plants and animals that require enormous expertise to understand. If you see a hummingbird hawk moth just once in your life, you'll never forget it, and it's not hard to find out what it's called. They're unavoidable, the butterflies on warm, sunny days, the moths at dusk and later.

Summer nights are a story of their own. You can collect almost anything at night – except flies. A hover-fly at night is as inconceivable as a swallow.

The only thing I can collect at night is my own thoughts.

A theory. Some aspects of a person's fundamental nature are inherited in the usual, prosaic fashion – musicality, intelligence, genetic diseases, and so forth – whereas there is no better explanation for others than early childhood imprinting in a particular environment. We needn't go into it deeply. There is no black and white. The outlines are diffuse. But I think we can assume that certain characteristics of what becomes a person are cultural artifacts rather than the boring, unfair consequences of cast-iron biology. One of these, I believe, is a pronounced romantic temperament. Maybe not completely, but mostly.

My next observation is equally banal, namely, that we in Sweden have the world's loveliest summer nights. Even a short distance down into Europe the nights become gloomy, pitch-black conveyances from dusk to dawn. Tropical nights can build into tremendous explosions of downright Cambro-Silurian cacophony when a thunderstorm starts or cicadas celebrate their orgies in the treetops. They're magnificent, but no more than that. The indescribable sound of the Madagascar nightjar is worth the entire trip, but in the end it is merely interesting and exciting and fun to tell people about later. It doesn't come close to the endless beauty of a summer night in Sweden.

Every summer there are a number of nights, not many, but a number, when everything is perfect. The light, the warmth, the smells, the mist, the birdsong – the moths. Who can sleep? Who wants to?

Most people do, it seems. As for me, I'm on the verge of tears from happiness, and I wander around on the island till dawn and dream and think that summer nights are our most under-utilized natural resource. The thought is new, but the dreams and the wanderings have gone on for as long as I can remember. For in the superficially darling town by the sea on the outskirts of which I had my childhood, I was the only kid allowed to run free at night. You can't send a moth-hunter to bed, no matter how young he is. And my parents were – still are – touchingly unsuspecting people who never even considered the possibility that their little boy did anything but catch moths under the nearest streetlamp.

I was constantly out at night. I listened for marsh warblers, spied on badgers, stole strawberries and threw pine cones at girls' windows. Of course I also collected moths, lots of them, and was almost always alone. It was only when I was older that I rode my bike into town and drank like a Polish translator, but that's not relevant here. The imprinting was already irrevocable.

Ever since, I have regarded all warmish summer

147

nights as my personal property. Sadly enough, I never have to share them with a lot of people other than Frithiof and sometimes a large toad that lives under the porch and every summer comes out to the corner of the cottage where I hang up a bed sheet in front of the moth lamp. We sit at opposite ends of the sheet as if it were a tablecloth. The toad always catches more than I do. Frithiof tells me how it used to be.

Of course it's lonely at times. It would be silly to deny it.

'When you go to study the insect world, you need to prepare much within yourself as well,' wrote Harry Martinson, and the first thing entomologists must prepare themselves for is loneliness. I imagine that's why the typical entomologist concentrates on butterflies or moths. Enough people know enough about them to make that activity more or less meaningful in a social context. Finding people with a similar bent is not impossible, and even if the collector usually has to work alone, his finest finds are so pretty that anyone at all can understand his pleasure and share it. Everyone knows what a death's head hawk moth looks like, or a swallowtail. OK, not everyone, but enough to satisfy the collector's need for companionship.

The fly expert, on the other hand, usually plugs away in vain. For me, a *Doros profuges* is like a death's head hawk moth, but for almost no one else. A mass invasion of *Eristalis similis* is a sensation. How many people were there who even noticed? Five?

To be sure, there is a forum on the internet that links people with similar interests all over the world, but ever since the Americans bombed Serbia I have the feeling it's being censored. In any case, the discussions have become less interesting and too narrowly scientific since then. That's too bad, because it could have been a breathing hole for us amateurs, too.

It was in March 1999. The bombers were fuelled and ready at their bases. They were all just waiting for the order to take off. And then a message appeared on the fly forum website from one of Europe's leading hoverfly experts, a Serbian. It was just a short greeting, thanking everyone for their participation at the last international meeting. Nothing political. He wrote only that he was at home waiting for the bombs. And then he wished everyone good luck in their lives. That was all. The next day there were expressions of sympathy from his friends in other countries and for a moment it really felt as if we were connected. But on day three there came a message from one of the really big men in the field, from the Smithsonian Institution in Washington. He wrote that we should all settle down, stick to the subject of insects, and keep politics out of it. (Although his was the only remotely political message.) Anyway, that was the end of that. Global conversations in open forums are rarely very rewarding, not even about flies.

Little by little, our correspondence came to resemble those scanty concerts you can sometimes hear on an early spring evening when three or four pygmy owls sit whistling to each other. They're far apart but still close enough to clearly mark their territories.

And so we help one another as best we can within the country. I have two friends who know more about hoverflies than I. That goes a long way. As soon as I catch something worth shouting about, I notify them and they always send me back an email with congratulations and an adequate pinch of envy. And then there are all the other entomologists who know less about flies than other insects, but they often know enough. They understand the thrill. The way Frithiof does, and Sten, René, Harry and all the others who are dead but nevertheless still here.

Chapter 11

The Fly Tree

There was once a giant tree, in Ronneby of all places, that Linnaeus in his writings called the Fly Tree. In fact it was called that long before Linnaeus. Its history can explain why we search and search for certain flies without ever seeing them – the legendary insects, as I think we might call them.

I am speaking now of the almost mythical hover-flies – large and beautiful – whose larvae pass their days in water-filled cavities high in the crowns of trees. You can spend a lifetime searching for them, so rare are they.

The Fly Tree was one of the largest trees that ever grew in Sweden, a black poplar that dated from the Middle Ages. Until 1884, it rose above the court-house by the Ronneby River like a grey-green cumulus cloud. The trunk was eleven metres in circumference; the largest of its limbs a good five. An oil barrel has a circumference of about two metres, so you can imagine its size. So gigantic was this tree that the citizens of Ronneby bragged about it as a marvel of oriental dimensions, the sort of thing you put on picture postcards and send off in all directions. There was no one for a hundred miles who didn't know that this giant was called the Fly Tree. It was an entire ecosystem. For example, somewhere in the midst of this eruption of limbs and greenery, home to entire flocks of jackdaws, was a fork at the bottom of which they found what came to be called a spring. It was undoubtedly filled with the larvae of the legendary insects, although that was not how the tree got its name. It was called the Fly Tree because every autumn, especially after summers with a lot of rain, the crown was transformed literally into a cloud – of swarming aphids. Clearly, one or more species of gall-generating aphid lived in the tree, in small nodes on leaf stems, and because the whole spectacle was of such unearthly size, and the aphids so cosmically numerous, the whole thing became, over the course of centuries, a recurring annual event, strange and horrible enough to write about on the picture postcards.

Unfortunately, one limb broke in a downpour in 1882, whereupon some boorish bureaucrat in the city got the idea that the tree stood in the way of progress – in exactly what way is unknown. At the same time a rumour began to spread that the trunk was so rotten to its very marrow that the whole colossus had to be taken down. And so it was. The longest saws were sharpened. It's small comfort now that they were wrong about the rot. The trunk turned out to be sound to the core, and it's pleasing to note that it refused to be cut down in an afternoon. In fact, it refused to be cut down at all. The Fly Tree withstood all attempts to fell it.

Except dynamite. And that's how the story ends. They blew it to bits with dynamite. For the sake, alas, of progress.

Some insects are so secretive throughout their lives that only a few specimens are seen in the course of a century, and it may be that one or two hoverflies fall into that category. Another possibility is that they are no longer with us, because the really fabulous trees are gone or anyway far fewer in number.

In our garden on the island we have a number of trees with the potential to grow huge over the years – an oak, an ash, several maples, poplars, alders, birches and some pines, of course, plus a fir by the lake that seems to suffer from some odd genetic disorder that makes it look like a gigantic pipe cleaner. It grows a foot every summer (some mornings it looks like the antenna on a transistor radio), and since it's in an exposed location, the north wind will probably take it down some day. In the long run, probably only the oak and the ash will survive, but since the oak is no more than maybe a hundred years old and the ash is hardly fifty, it will be a lifetime or two before they attain the right internal consistency.

I'm putting my hopes instead on one of the maples, a pretty tree that someone levelled with the ground a long time ago but that was then allowed to put out stump shoots in peace. Consequently it has eight trunks, not especially thick but all growing in a ring around a hole left by the original stump, now long since rotted away. This hollow is always filled with about a litre and a half of brownish sludge. As if it were a waterhole on the savannah. I sit by it for hours and wait. So far nothing has happened.

There are a number of other stumps where I spend late summer days, mostly poplars, some of them as tall as houses. Poplars can grow very large, as everyone knows, but they are still rather unstable. They just grow too fast. On top of which their wood is soft enough that woodpeckers can rip a hole in them and nest. Pretty much all of the older poplars on the island have been invaded by woodpeckers, and afterwards the trunk becomes more or less hollow from fungal decay and thus a suitable spawning place for rare hoverflies. In the end, the large poplars grow sort of tired, tip to one side, and eventually fall over. Unless, of course, a storm takes them down first. That happens, especially with poplars, and what remains are giant stumps, which stand for decades and entertain woodpeckers, tawny owls, beetles, wasps, hoverflies – and me.

You can even make good politics out of a well-placed

stump. A friend of mine on the mainland did just that several years ago, and as far as I can tell, his opponents haven't recovered yet. It was the usual stuff. They wanted to scare up a bunch of rare species – lichens, fungi, insects, all sorts of things – to use as brickbats in some tribal war between different bureaucracies. In short, if memory serves, they were asking for money to buy more nature reserves. Something like that. An old story – and a fine idea, except for the fact that the people organizing the whole thing were so hopelessly lost to the idea that 'good' nature must necessarily be untouched, or at least look as if it had been clipped from a fairy tale by Astrid Lindgren.

Seven municipalities joined forces and for three years they inventoried almost 500 wild areas of a suitable type. Naturally they found a lot of what they were looking for.

My friend, who is a carpenter but also an inventive entomologist, began a study of his own at about the same time, and in one of the same general areas. His goal may not necessarily have been to hog-tie the army of municipal bean counters, but he did want to remind them that damaged environments, too, can be rich in rare species. So while all the other field workers were tramping about in the wilderness, capturing specimens till they were blue in the face, he put a ladder over his shoulder and walked out to a clear-cut forest where he knew there was a lonely 25-foot poplar stump. He then made an inventory of its insects.

He kept at it for several years, collecting on one stump in a cut-over forest that no one else cared to study because it had already been destroyed. Oddly enough, he found nearly as many endangered insects on his stump as all the other inventory-takers together found on almost one hundred square kilometres.

What's less amusing is that our environmental politics are themselves a natural disaster, tipping over and threatening to fall. Positions are locked and the investments often so great that anyone who makes a careless statement about the legendary insects in the very epicentre of a devastated area must be prepared to make friends they don't want. But things are never as simple as they look, unfortunately, so when everything is said and done we shouldn't draw any conclusion other than that some efforts to measure nature are more elegant than others, if not necessarily better. Or at least they're quieter. As usual, it's all a matter of context. The stump stands like an island in the clear-cut desolation. And as Ralph says in *Lord of the Flies*, 'This is our island. It's a good island. Until the grown-ups come to fetch us we'll have fun.'

As long as there have been biologists, they have sought out islands to keep profusion from making them crazy. Islands are generalizations of a kind. Explanatory models. And where there are no islands, we have to invent them. If only for the fun of it.

. . .

Once you've developed an eye for them, you see them everywhere – synthetic islands in the archipelago of buttonology. One of the finest is in Rome, or rather *was* in Rome, in the mid-1800s. A defined paradise in the midst of that great, teeming, confusing metropolis. Richard Deakin was the name of the man who invented it. He was a doctor, and let us suppose that he worked hard at his career, hard enough to need relaxation and distraction. We can also suppose that, as a doctor, he knew well enough that opium was no long-term solution. But he needed something, a lifeboat of some kind. I don't really know, but I'm guessing that's roughly what happened.

What I do know about Deakin's life is in fact very meagre. I have tried to do some research, but he is largely forgotten, even in his own country, remembered principally by aged botanists and dusty collectors of rare books with hand-coloured plates. All I really know is that he was an Englishman who, in his free time, studied the distribution of plants. Among other things, he wrote about British ferns. I have no idea how he happened to move his medical practice to Rome. But he did, and he obviously took his passion for flora with him.

In a rare-book shop, I happened to catch sight of his name embossed in faded gold on a wine-red book with the inconsequential title *Flora of Rome*. Aha, I thought, a city flora. Urban biology is in many ways a fruitful subject, tantalizing in its unpredictability, so I opened the book and found to my delight that it was not at all the sort of plant guide I had expected but rather the story of a desert island, a sort of botanical Robinsoniana in an urban setting. Published in 1855. The complete title was *Flora of the Colosseum of Rome; or, illustrations and descriptions of four hundred and twenty plants growing spontaneously upon the ruins of the Colosseum of Rome.*

As I said, the facts are missing, but let us suppose that Dr Deakin had his hands full at his job. Perhaps he supported a large family. What to do? Long walks on Sunday to enjoy the views was not his cup of tea. He wanted to botanize, to jump from rock to rock around an island and collect plants and then catalogue them.

He solved his problem brilliantly. He made an inventory of a ruin.

He spent his free time clambering about in the Colosseum, happy as a child, and in light of how much he found, he must have been at it for years. He even described an unknown species, a grass that he named *Festuca romana*, and he found flowers that no one before him had ever seen in all of Italy. Since he wanted to share his finds (and himself) with the world, he bottled his childish delight in a book – which, in contrast to many other works in that genre, is still readable. Certain strange species from distant lands give him an opportunity to philosophize about the ruin's violent history, while others tempt him out into the morass of legends and old folklore where all botanizing authors eventually gather. Nightshade and crown of thorns are plants worthy of their own books. Or *Narcissus poeticus*, which no one escapes. Only Shelley can help Deakin here:

> *And narcissi, the fairest among them all,*
> *Who gaze on their eyes in the stream's recess,*
> *Till they die of their own dear loveliness.*

I can't help being envious. What poet writes verses in honour of the narcissus fly? Or of any hoverfly at all? World literature may be full of flies, but they are almost always anonymous – just flies. Hoverflies are mentioned here and there, yes. Martinson does it, Sven Barthel and Chatwin, but never ever are they permitted to step forth from the formless crowd, as species with names and histories. It's not so strange. Not even I can get upset about it. Just envious of all the birds and flowers and butterflies. Entire libraries abound in them. All of literature.

We show up literally in the undergrowth.

Worst of all, the names don't even work as names. The fact that hoverfly people use Latin all the time does not make the situation better. *Helophilus*, *Melanostoma*, *Xylota*. In the best of cases, a layperson can get a vague picture of how these small creatures live or what they look like, but usually the names tell them absolutely nothing. It's all a foreign language, literally. The only really housebroken names are the occasional scientific designations that have their origins in love of the normal, comprehensible kind, that is to say, in cases where the entomologist in question has christened some bug after his wife or maybe his mistress. It's not uncommon, and then the mists lift for a moment for whoever is listening. The name clings to the material world like a burdock.

'Check and see if he named any hymenoptera after her. In that case, it was true love.'

I'd been asking around about René Malaise, and now I was sitting with a professional entomologist on the line, a man who'd come up with some curious names himself over the years. We'd been talking about Ester Blenda Nordström, speculating pretty freely about why they married. It was then he suggested that I check the hymenoptera. That a marriage of convenience might lead to Latin names was out of the question, he thought, but as soon as deeper feelings were involved, anything was possible. He had himself recently named a beetle only four millimetres long in honour of his wife, so he was speaking from experience.

'Look through the insects from Kamchatka. That's where you'll find your answer.'

And how I looked! I spent an entire day at the museum poring over articles about all the new species René had brought home from the Far East, and some of the writing was so dry it might have burst into flame. There were some undeniably interesting items, hymenoptera with names like *bergmani*, *hulténi*, *hedstroemi* and *sjoeblomi*, that last one named for the engineer Karl Sjöblom, who lived with René and Ester Blenda in Klyutchi in the mid-1920s. The only person missing was, in fact, Ester Blenda. On the other hand, that may not be significant, because he didn't organize this material until the 1930s, by which time the marriage had already been dissolved.

In any case, as long as I was there I took the opportunity to glance through some other articles from a different trip Malaise made later – to Burma. And there! *Nordströmia amabilis*. But no, it wasn't her. This insect, a butterfly new to science, was named after Frithiof, not Ester Blenda, and the man who described it (and was therefore entitled to name it whatever he wanted) was another of the period's entomological madmen. His name was Felix Bryk (1882–1957) and he had a number of strings to his bow. Among other things, he travelled in Africa and wrote a clearly X-rated book called *Neger-Eros: Etnologische Studien über das Sexualleben bei Negern* (1928), but that needn't concern us here.

As usual, what I found in the end was not what I was looking for. *Ebba soederhalli*. A sawfly from Burma. Malaise had finally found love. An unmistakable case.

Chapter 12

The Entomologist's Career

René Malaise never had children. The memories were dispersed along with the heritage. Isn't it strange how far a person like Malaise can sink into oblivion in the course of only a few decades? And yet he carved his mark as well as he could. Even his legacies were generous: the insects; his property in Roslagen, north of Stockholm; his incomparable art collection in the villa on Lidingö.

I looked up his nephews and nieces. Friendly people with bright recollections of a man whose renown belonged to a completely different age, a dotty relative who'd gone his own way, always in the same good spirits. They smiled in amazement and a kind of embarrassment when I told them that every entomologist everywhere knows his name, if only in the form of a trap. His siblings and their children had called him Puppan, no one knew exactly why. It was just a nickname of the kind people in every family have in readiness for particularly eccentric relatives.

They searched in every corner and attic for half-forgotten memories and traces. They lent me everything they found. Yellowed newspaper clippings, some letters, a bundle of postcards, his passport, photographs. Not much.

But in any case, I learned enough to understand that his heyday was the 1930s. It's true that at times I was inclined to regard his whole life as a single unbroken heyday, because I think that's the way he saw it himself. But if we evaluate his importance as a minor celebrity and public personality, successful in the eyes of other people, then it's the 30s that are his.

He went home. Why? No one knows. His return to Sweden remains as unexplained as his reasons for spending pretty much the entire 1920s in Kamchatka. Maybe the bureaucracy became too troublesome. His

Soviet trade-union book, which still exists, was issued in 1929. It is full of stamps and cryptic notations, and one of the attic discoveries is a couple of badly dog-eared but legible certificates regulating the sable catch he lived on periodically. I can readily imagine that Malaise, or 'Citizen M' as he's called in the documents, was not really happy with the way the Kamchatka district agricultural administration rode hard on him. He abandoned his Kamchatka adventure and left the tundra for good. Maybe he was simply ready to leave.

After several months of intensive hymenoptera-hunting outside Vladivostok in the summer of 1930, he took the train to Stockholm.

How he supported himself over the next few years is not known, but there is reason to believe that he lived on a combination of inherited money, lecture fees, grants, and research fellowships from the Academy of Science and other institutions. It was only in 1938 that he took a position in the entomological department of the National Museum of Natural History, where he remained until 1958. But let's not get ahead of our story. Let's begin with his career. Which was brilliant.

First and foremost, Malaise was a collector. There can be no doubt about that. He had the necessary imagination and, above all, the persistence, the inexhaustible energy. But in contrast to so many other talented collectors, he was also energetic and productive when it came to organizing and systematizing his catch with scientific rigour. A flood of pedantic texts on the taxonomy of sawflies began to appear in scientific journals, and the first part of his classification table of the sawfly species that occur in Sweden, still in use, appeared as early as 1931.

It was also at this time, 1933, that he married Ebba Söderhell, a teacher of biology and religion at Lidingö High School. And the fact that he named a Burmese sawfly after her should not be misinterpreted. We must understand it – according to the prevalent custom among entomologists – as love.

Now there are those who insist that our hero had in the meantime entered into a second marriage of convenience, with the writer Vivi Laurent. But I've done a good deal of research in this matter, and I've been unable to find evidence for anything more than a close friendship. Frankly, I think this relationship is a family rumour that has been blown out of proportion over the years. Maybe it was René himself who invented the whole story. It wouldn't surprise me. They *could* have been married. According to the legend, spelled out in a little biography of Malaise that was printed or rather stencilled in a handful of copies, the idea behind the marriage was that they were going to Egypt together. Once there, however, Vivi paired up with the botanist Gunnar Täckholm (whom she demonstrably did marry), whereupon René is supposed to have come home. As I said, however, I don't believe the rumour is true.

I mention it anyway, partly because life on the island has taught me to appreciate hearsay, partly because the friendship with Vivi, however close it may or may not have been, may tell us something about René Malaise. For example, that he was drawn to strong, independent, adventurous women. Long before Vivi Laurent-Täckholm became an honoured and world-renowned professor of botany at the University of Cairo, she enjoyed great success as a young writer, much the same way Ester Blenda Nordström did, and partly with the same kind of daring, caustic social reporting. They truly had much in common, although their destinies were incomparably different. For one thing, Vivi lived as long as René. At his eightieth birthday party in 1972, there she is making her way through the crowd. I've seen the photograph.

Undeniably, Ebba Malaise makes a somewhat more restful impression. But only somewhat. She was not one to sit at home in Stockholm and knit while her husband saw the world. On the contrary. The year they were married she went along happily on the poorly financed and, to say the least, dangerous expedition to Burma, and there, in the wilderness, it was often her contributions that made the trip such a great success.

Malaise, in short, had not had enough. He was an explorer, after all, and he had truly mastered the art of travelling. Several years at a microscope had been very quiet, perhaps, but they had shown him that a really pioneering dissertation on Asiatic sawflies would necessitate further collecting expeditions in addition to those he had made to the Soviet Union. And the whitest areas on the biologists' maps were in northern Burma and in the neighbouring province of Yunnan in southern China. That's where he'd go. There he would test his ingenious trap. He had demonstrated the invention both in Stockholm and at the British Museum in London, although most people had just laughed at him. They had the greatest faith in him as a specimen collector, but the fly trap was considered a joke. In time, it would prove to be anything but.

The Burma expedition was a fairly brief excursion, at least by his standards. It lasted from the end of 1933 to the beginning of 1935. Nevertheless, it was a triumph, thanks in great part to the traps he had sewn in Rangoon. They exceeded all expectations, even his own. In addition, he managed with Ebba's help to transform all the village children into field assistants, as tireless as he himself. It was Ebba who ran the pharmacy, and her renown as a healer spread rapidly in that wild country. In a description of the journey that he wrote for the journal *Ymer*, René writes:

People often appeared with all sorts of lizards, snakes,
household utensils, and anything else they thought
we might want, and every morning when the sick
bay was completed, all the children in the village
would come, each with a little bamboo tube, and
when they took out the wad of moss in one end and
tipped out the contents, I had to make a quick grab for
the scampering beetles, centipedes, or whatever else
they'd had in their bamboo shoots.

They had set up base in Kambaiti, a small village 2,000 metres above sea level in the northeast corner of the country, a stone's throw from the Chinese border and not far from the headwaters of the Mekong River. It was virgin country, wild in every sense of the word. The rain forest was pretty much untouched, the insect life was almost completely unknown, and the people who lived there in the mountains had only recently given up headhunting and other customs so barbaric that the British, the colonial authorities, had prevailed upon Malaise to give them a written assurance that he travelled the area at his own risk.

René had been through this before. Afraid he was not – not of savages nor of miserable living conditions in smoky huts with mouldy floors and leaky roofs. And, however it happened, it seems that Ebba was made of the same stuff. One of her tasks in Burma was to buy and trade for ethnographic objects – costumes, weapons, musical instruments, pieces of art, tools of every description – and a look at the result (the collection is in the Museum of World Culture in Gothenburg) shows that she must have thrown herself into the adventure without much hesitation. One day they crossed the border into China:

> Only a few kilometres on the other side of the border we discovered that the official warning was not entirely unjustified. Our boy was walking ahead of us when he was suddenly stopped by three mountain tribesmen. One of them was armed with a rifle, which he pointed at the boy's chest. But when the man caught sight of my wife and me, he lowered the rifle and waited to see what would happen. Our boy was unarmed, but I had a revolver in my pocket and a

shotgun on my back. As we approached, the boy took
the opportunity to move away, but when my wife
saw the tribesman's rifle, it aroused her ethnographic
interest and she walked up to examine it more closely.
This made me uneasy, for if it came to hostilities, she
stood directly in my line of fire and would have kept
me from shooting. She apparently understood the
danger, for she pulled a butterfly jar from her pocket,
showed it to the three men, and spoke to them, as
usual, in Swedish.

Swedish schoolteacher with dead butterfly in jar. Not surprisingly, the bandits were utterly befuddled.

When the monsoon rains rendered all further specimen collection in the mountains impossible, they headed south to the Shan States – closer to the northern border of Thailand and difficult to reach even today – into the area now called the Golden Triangle. René moved ahead like a thrashing machine with his net. Ebba traded for hundreds of objects, including a canoe. You have to wonder how they dealt with all the baggage.

. . .

Is it energy that's the secret? Perseverance? Can it be that simple?

I myself just get tired and gloomy, sometimes apathetic. The last thing I want is adventure. And, least of all, people speaking a language I don't understand. The easiest days are when I meet a fellow Swede, as if the invisible codes of language and culture were the combination to a lock. I am forever sitting around the hotel or the hostel. At a café, a bar. The first such place where I became a 'regular' was in Ouagadougou. Always a regular. If I'm in a city for only a week, I find a place to go back to. Before the week is out, I don't even need to order. They know what I want. The usual.

How can you long to go back to a place before you've even been there?

. . .

Their homecoming was grand. A media event. 'Distinguished Scientist and Wife Return from Burma and South China', cried one newspaper on its front page. Another headline declared 'Dr Malaise and Wife

Home Today'. In Gothenburg, there was wild rejoicing at the wonderful collection of *ethnographica*, unique in the world, and at the National Museum of Natural History in Stockholm, which was to share the insects with the British Museum, they were prostrate with admiration and respect.

If there had been a great deal of material to organize after the Kamchatka expedition, it was nothing compared with what the entomology department now unpacked. Over time, the specimens would be sorted, prepared, labelled and sent to experts all over the world, family by family, genus by genus, species by species, endlessly. Still today, seventy years later, they haven't seen the bottom of every jar (which is probably scandalous) and the number of scientific articles the Burmese insects have given rise to is difficult to estimate.

Because so much was new to science, a number of species were named after their eminent collector. Just among the click beetles, a relatively small family, there are thirteen Burmese species in different genera with the species name *malaisei*. In addition, he managed to bring home 1,700 fresh-water fish in formalin, which he seems to have grabbed almost absent-mindedly in the frenzy of collecting.

He gave interviews, delivered lectures on the radio, and appeared at every conceivable kind of event whenever he wasn't doing research or publishing articles. He now began in earnest to work on his magnum opus on sawflies, and of course to prepare his next expedition – to Ceylon, southern India and the western Himalayas. Attracting financial backing was no trouble this time, for he was now once and for all an established explorer. His renown had spread far beyond narrow scientific circles, indeed all the way to the weeklies and the daily verses of the major newspapers. Some doggerel from *Dagens Nyheter* may say more about his position in society at that time than all the praise pouring in from scientists all over the world.

> *As the Far Eastern earth surface trembles,*
> *as volcanoes erupt near and far,*
> *The Doctor examines a sawfly,*
> *which he quietly stuffs in a jar.*

As bandits approach him in China
*   with rifle and pistol and knife,*
He places a bug in a test tube
*   and sits down to study its life.*
But high in the mountains of Asia,
*   beyond reach of man or machine,*
Dwell sawflies and buglets aplenty
*   that he never, no, never has seen.*
So that's where he longs to escape to,
*   and that's where his plan is to flee*
From the poplar-tree sawflies of Sweden,
*   from the song of the native-born bee.*

Every last detail had been seen to and the departure date set for 4 November 1939. It was then the boat would leave. But the war got in the way. The plan fell to pieces. Burma was his last expedition. He bought himself a house in the Stockholm archipelago instead, in Simpnäs, some way up the coast, and by the time the war was over in 1945, he was consumed by other interests.

The age of Linnaeus and Nordenskiöld was over. Exploration had changed. In the first place, the world lay in ruins, and later, in the 50s, it was the turn of the nature film-makers to become the popular heroes in search of distant lands. Innumerable scientific expeditions to collect nameless creepy-crawlies have sailed in the years since then, of course, but the lustre and honour have never really returned. Journeys that were public business before the war are now carried out in silence. Adventurers don't even make films any more, they just have adventures, as if the Himalayas were an obstacle course for ambitious men who would never dream of making a torturous detour by way of the incomprehensible taxonomy of sawflies.

Chapter 13

Slowness

The island's population increases tenfold in the summer – three thousand people in varying states of freedom. At first you don't see them, for at the start of their holidays they stay in their summer houses with their families, often several generations together. This lasts no more than a couple of weeks at most, or until life in these usually small cottages grows unsustainable and begins to become as threatening as something in a play by Lars Norén. That's when the long walks begin in earnest. My image as a fly collector is in many ways a product of this phenomenon – because I answer the questions these restless wanderers ask about what I'm doing and why.

As long as the wild chervil is in bloom, everything is fine, because it grows everywhere and I know some remote spots, ideal for hoverflies, where no other person ever ventures. But when the raspberry thickets bloom and the thistles and the spirea, then I have to stand closer to the roads and the questions.

You get used to it. But sometimes, on certain days, the nicest days, when there are a lot of people out and about, I get tired of explaining and start lying instead, like a hitchhiker. They almost always lie, at least on the main roads, for the simple reason that otherwise they'd get sick of their own history. It can be very taxing to stick to the truth for a whole day, in maybe a dozen different cars, answering the same questions about where you're going and why. That's why hitchhikers live such interesting lives. It's all lies. The same is true of fly-collectors whom people will not leave in peace.

'What are you doing?'

'Catching butterflies.'

That's the cheapest lie. It almost always works extremely well and does not lead to follow-up questions. I believe that the butterfly-hunter is seen as a somewhat touching figure, delicate and a little pathetic, a person who ought to be left there in the sunshine without further comment. Just a motherly smile and, tops, an encouraging 'I see'. No one needs to ask what a butterfly is, and everyone knows there are grown men who collect them.

However, it is not entirely risk-free, the butterfly lie. If your luck is bad, the person who disturbs your peace may be one of those increasingly common individuals who believe that all butterflies are protected by law and that consequently the collector is a criminal, possibly a pervert. In that case, the dialogue by the side of the road can be both long and tiresome, and in the meantime the flies are flying and so is the time.

'I'm collecting hoverflies' is an equally risky answer. Primarily because it's inadequate. On hearing the word hoverfly, every relatively normal Swede thinks of those small, enervating flies of quite different families, fruit flies mostly, that circulate indoors, even in winter,

among the potted plants. It generally goes something
like this:

'Flies!?'

'Yes, hoverflies.'

'Boy, you ought to come over to our place. We've
got masses of them.'

So then you have to clear up that misunderstand-
ing. It takes a while. And once you've said A you have
to say B, whereupon you're quickly drawn into a
whole seminar about the natural history of hoverflies,
their evolution, for example, and their importance for
pollination, as well as the uses and joys and technical
practicalities of hoverfly-collecting, not to mention
everything else that has any connection with flies or
insects or nature in general. The conversation glides
along and suddenly you're standing there with your
hands on your hips, philosophizing freely about the
prospects for a good mushroom season. It can be pleasant, it really can, and it can bring some days to a close
with a productive exchange of views about the modern
era's lack of leisure and contemplation. But no flies are
caught.

How easily we're transformed into dancers when someone is willing to listen.

'I'm collecting hoverflies' can also be taken as an absurd joke, or, worse yet, as a base provocation. I'll never forget the youngish man who came along on his bicycle one day when I found myself dangerously close to the road. It was when the bishop's weed was blooming in the drainage ditches, so there weren't a lot of really good places to choose from. Roads, gardens, refuse heaps, all of them hazardous places – socially, I mean – but bishop's weed is absolutely unbeatable for collecting flies so I usually grit my teeth and take the risk. The man caught sight of me and braked so hard the gravel flew. A tourist on a rented bike, wearing an open Hawaiian shirt. From the corner of my eye, I saw the way he was looking at me.

'What the hell are you doing?'

His tone was not exactly unfriendly, but I could tell right away that he felt compelled to deliver some observations, as if I were a communal tourist attraction, an EU-financed aborigine placed in the terrain exclusively as a form of outdoor entertainment. Such things apparently exist. Nevertheless, I told it like it was, and since I had just netted a couple of specimens of the magnificent hoverfly *Temnostoma vespiforme*, I handed him my poison jar in order to finish my hoverfly lecture as quickly as possible. He gave my catch a quick glance, handed the bottle back to me, and said: 'Those are wasps.'

'Yes, so you might think,' I said, and explained politely about mimicry, whereupon he asked to have another look. I handed back the jar, and this time he studied them long and hard in thoughtful silence.

'Those are wasps.'

His tone was now slightly irritated. I stuffed the jar in my pocket. Presumably he thought I was having a little fun with him, or else he simply wasn't used to being contradicted.

The situation was never threatening, more like comic. He lowered the kickstand on his bike, stationed himself with his legs wide apart and his arms crossed over his chest and fixed me with his gaze, as if awaiting my retreat in the face of an intellectually and morally and in every other respect superior opponent.

I attempted a neutral smile. No reaction. In fact, he looked a little angry. I decided instead to ignore him, but he stood where he was, immovable. He stood there like that for several minutes, trying to come up with a decisive final word. It was: 'Wasps! And don't you forget it!'

And then he cycled away, his Hawaiian shirt flapping in the breeze.

. . .

I borrowed the dancer from Milan Kundera. He uses the expression in an elegant comedy about vanity, ambition and the lust for power – just a short dialogue, in simple scenes, that breaks out here and there in a short novel called, precisely, *Slowness*. Well, novel is possibly not the right word to describe it, but it is in any case charming and as double-bottomed as an oil tanker. To be honest, I have never really understood what the book is about, but as with 'The Man Who Loved Islands', I was very taken with it before I knew much more than that it existed.

As with Lawrence, I was satisfied for years just

to know that a theme that interested me was also of interest to a man of Kundera's calibre. Moreover, I had, as usual, some theories of my own.

Slowness was quite simply a theme granted me by nature.

No, come to think of it, that's not true. It was the summer people who, with their questions, turned slowness into a theme granted me by nature. I had simply told one of them in a moment of inspiration that my fly-collecting was a method of exercising slowness. And because that comment was met with an understanding I'm not accustomed to, I continued using that answer and developed my theory later. The reactions were always effusive. As soon as I raised the subject, it was as if everyone in the whole world was, deep down, a fly-collector, though they had never realized it before. Some of them had read entire books about slowness and could hold long monologues about the excellence of everything slow.

At the time, I had never discovered that fascination, maybe because I am a rather slow person and had always wished that I was a bit faster. Now, quite unexpectedly,

I had become a pioneer in the field. It felt good. I listened eagerly to these summer people fleeing from family life and to their almost feverish lectures about the way our whole age is infected with speed. Communications are faster than ever, the news cycle too. People talk faster, eat faster, change opinions more often, experience more stress, while at the same time the whole world is being transformed at a breakneck pace. The speed of technological development is absolutely sensational, new models of innumerable devices literally pour out on to the market and all of them are faster than the ones that poured out last year, or just six months ago. Computers take the prize, of course, and telephones, but even toasters are now so fast they're approaching the critical limit where the bread gets brown on the surface before it's warm in the middle. And let's not even talk about the markets in currencies and securities.

'Yes, it's terrible,' I used to say, and make a few swipes with my net.

This apparently universal, self-generating acceleration does clearly create discomfort and concern of many kinds, and I was always happy to agree.

But to tell the truth, I still think it would be worse the other way around. If everything just got slower and slower we'd all go pretty much nuts and beg for speed with a sincerity that the preachers of slowness never come close to. If nothing else, the trend towards more and more, faster and faster, is preferable to its opposite because you can always get off an express train but there's no good way to speed up a donkey caravan. What's more, everyone has the freedom not to travel and in that way protect themselves from a lot of indigestible impressions and barbaric languages. If you think the torrent – of pictures, messages, people, whatever – goes too fast, then in nine cases out of ten you can turn it off or just close your eyes and breathe your own air for a while. Most of it is optional. That's the wonderful significance of Swedish prosperity.

But I didn't usually say all that to the summer people.

Some of us can't keep up, it may be as simple as that. It's just too much. We notice it while we're still in school. And since the pipes we learn to dance to are carved by people who love speed and can tame the profusion, we lose our balance and sink into a sullen sense of inadequacy. Some of this can be ascribed to sordid commercialism, but not nearly all of it. Cultural life is a department store, as is science when glimpsed from a distance. Brilliance and speed, helter-skelter.

Slowness is not an end in itself − neither a virtue nor a defeat.

Next summer I think I'll say that my fly collecting is a way of exercising concentration. A focus so intense that I forget myself. Which is not always so easy on the dance floor of our time. Kundera was on to that. He begins at that end.

So, of course, I finally bought the book, got myself all comfortably situated in the shade on the jetty and thought, all right, now I will really roll around in truths about life, the kind I could readily apply to my own slow fly-hunting and to what was perhaps my even more indolent life on the island. I recognized myself at once, right on the first page, in a man who is

> *caught in a fragment of time cut off from both the past and the future; he is wrenched from the continuity of*

time; he is outside time; in other words, he is in a
state of ecstasy; in that state he is unaware of his age,
his wife, his children, his worries, and so he has no
fear, because the source of fear is in the future, and a
person freed of the future has nothing to fear.

That was it. Exactly.

The unfortunate part was merely that Kundera wasn't describing an indolent entomologist in this passage but a reckless motorcyclist in the midst of the perilous whirlpool of French traffic. In fact, it turns out that this irresponsible daredevil is the source of the author's reflections on slowness. Why, he asks, have the pleasures of slowness disappeared? 'Ah, where have they gone, the amblers of yesteryear?'

How disappointing. A little half-heartedly I glanced at the wormwood to check for *Volucella inanis* and considered not reading on, considered not reading any book with an enticing title ever again. In future I would just try instead to imagine the great truths they might contain. At the time, this seemed to be the most attractive solution. But then I went on reading anyway.

The hook was well baited. 'In our world, indolence has turned into having nothing to do, which is a completely different thing: a person with nothing to do is frustrated, bored, is constantly searching for the activity he lacks.'

This was different.

Moreover, it soon became clear that the book was mostly about sex.

The story begins with the author and his wife, Vera, out driving somewhere in the countryside outside Paris. They have just decided to spend the night in an old chateau that lies nearby, on the banks of the Seine, and on their way there they sit and chat about the reckless rush of the traffic, and about the way everyone is in a hurry and impatient, and about death. Like so many other French chateaux, this one has been turned into a hotel and has added a conference hall and a swimming pool since the last time they stayed here. But before they arrive, the story has already dissolved into at least two time schemes, and one of them takes place in the eighteenth century – to be precise, in and around Vivant Denon's erotic short story 'No Tomorrow'.

This is all a little hard to follow, and it gets even worse when Kundera starts pursuing a third trail, which is really a satire on French intellectuals, or, as mentioned earlier, a comedy where dancers enter the action. 'The dancer differs from the politician in that he seeks not power but glory; his desire is not to impose this or that social scheme on the world (he couldn't care less about that) but to take over the stage so as to beam forth his self.' As far as I can judge after many readings, this is the main theme of *Slowness*. The title alludes principally to the drawn-out arts of seduction that a certain Madame T. and her lover devote themselves to in Denon's short story. In any event, that book is about orgies very different from the ones I'm accustomed to conducting in the bushes. I understood that much when I was still on the dock in the shade.

But the morphology of ambition is as good a subject as any, I thought, and the dancers seemed to me strangely familiar, so I read on – and very nearly fell in the lake from astonishment when suddenly, without any warning at all, an old acquaintance strode right into the plot. Now it got exciting.

Oddly enough, the chateau, now a conference hotel, where Milan Kundera and his wife have just eaten their dinner and enjoyed a magnificent Bordeaux, is at this very moment hosting an entomological seminar. This meeting promptly melts into the fiction and becomes the scene of the dancers' and the seducers' tragicomic circus tricks, but at least one of the conferees is disguised so thinly that I recognized him at once. 'The room fills gradually; there are many French entomologists and a few from abroad, among them a Czech in his sixties . . .'

The novel tells us that this man, whose fate resembles Kundera's own, was a very successful scientist in Prague, a professor who worked exclusively with flies, until he fell into disfavour following the Soviet invasion of 1968, and after that, like so many other intellectuals, was forced to support himself as a construction worker.

He has now been away from his research for two decades, but he is nevertheless going to present a short paper on a fly, *Musca pragensis*, that he discovered and described in his youth. Nervously he waits his turn, thinking his lecture doesn't amount to much, but as soon as the moderator introduces him as the next speaker and he starts walking to the podium, he is gripped by a completely unexpected impulse. With tears in his eyes, he decides to follow his spontaneous urge and tell the group, briefly, about his fate – just a few introductory words about how happy he is to be back among his old friends. Not that he hadn't made friends in the building trade – but he missed the passion, the entomological passion.

And his audience is moved. They stand, applaud, film cameras are turned towards the Czech scientist, who weeps with joy. 'And he knows that right now he is living the greatest moment of his life, the moment of glory, yes, of glory, why not say the word, he feels grand and beautiful, he feels famous, and he wants his walk to his seat to be long and never-ending.'

He is so moved, this man, that he forgets to deliver his paper.

Milan Chvála! In the book he's called something else, but the character must be modelled on Milan Chvála. For a long time, Prague was a sort of capital city for European entomology, and Chvála was one of its really prominent figures, world famous among experts, the uncontested master of flies of many kinds ever since the 1960s. I myself have a number of his books on my shelves – his 500-page monograph on the European horse flies (family *Tabanidae*) and several volumes that treat what is perhaps his foremost specialty, *Empidoidae*, the family of flies that remarkably enough are called dance flies in Swedish.

'Every meeting has its deserters who gather in an adjoining room to drink.' Yes, the whole thing falls apart quite quickly, and since Kundera is Kundera, one of his dancing narcissists manages the utterly improbable (believe me) trick of conjuring up a woman to seduce from among this relatively ordinary gallery of fly-conference participants, 'because the real victory, the only one that counts, is the conquest of a woman picked up fast in the grimly unerotic milieu of the entomologists'.

I can vouch for that last part. Normally no women take part at all. And the few who do happen to show up are usually the better halves of the biggest crackpots, wives who could easily pass as personal assistants from a psychiatric open ward. Well, maybe that's unfair. But the fact is that unattached women could hardly find a better hunting ground than entomological societies. Unusual men, no competition. Just a suggestion.

Where was I? Of course – slowness.

A theme granted me by nature.

Which is probably just an unjustifiable simplification, a mental wild-goose chase, a poetic paraphrase meant to make a virtue of, or hide, a genetic inability to deal with choice. There is no need to question the fact that what the fly collector does is for purely practical reasons slow and sometimes stationary, but in the final analysis, the concentration and obliviousness that give him peace of mind have nothing to do with slowness. He could just as well be riding a motorcycle.

The art of limitation is altogether different, and probably not much of an art. All that's required is the courage to see your own mastery in actual life size. Some people see only flies, or certain flies, in a certain place, for a certain time. It's only a starting point, or a fixed point, but it is a point. That's all it is.

Chapter 14

The Island that Sank in the Sea

The history of biology has many stars, and two of them shine brighter than all the rest together – Carl Linnaeus and Charles Darwin. I don't know what kind of breakthrough it would take for someone, sometime, even to approach the power they exercise over the way we think about life on earth. Above all, Darwin strikes me as utterly impossible to surpass, so great is the truth he saw and described in the most complete detail. Of course, Linnaeus is also magnificent, but what makes him a megastar for ever is that he managed to sell an operating system, a bit like Bill Gates. What he didn't do was formulate an eternal truth.

Anyway, both Linnaeus and Darwin founded schools in their respective domains – classification and the theory of evolution. But their lives, too – the very chronology of their careers – became models for generations of natural scientists. First, the youthful travels. Thereafter, patient, narrowly focused research. Finally, the revolutionary ideas and the great books in repeated new editions. A myriad of biologists have managed to follow their example in the first two stages – the travels and the tunnel vision of specialized research. It's only in the final phase that the plan goes off track. René Malaise, I'm sorry to say, was no exception to this unhappy rule.

Or was he just unlucky?

Before turning a lens on his boldest ideas, however, let's pause for a moment with the two empire builders, if only to note another interesting similarity between them – the fact that they were not alone. Neither Linnaeus nor Darwin was as monolithically exceptional as posterity has been pleased to represent him. As regards the theory of evolution, this fact is well known. Right from the outset, Alfred Russel Wallace, the young collector working in the archipelagos of southeast Asia, was recognized as having formulated the same idea as Darwin. In certain respects, he was actually the more original of the two, but he was not as comprehensive as the old man at Down House. Moreover, he was not at home when the race was run.

Less well known is the fact that Linnaeus was not alone either. It's a long story, and I won't go into all of it here. Just observe that there is almost always someone else in the background. In Linnaeus's case, his name was Peter Artedi (1705–1735). They were best friends as students in Uppsala. Peter was two years older, born in Anundsjö in Ångermanland, and knew at least as much natural history as the little man from Stenbrohult. Together they developed the great system. Not each of them separately, like Wallace and Darwin, but together, over years of intensive collaboration. And it was Artedi, I believe, who was the real genius. Tragically, however, he drowned in one of Amsterdam's canals, only thirty years of age. He probably took his own life. The spotlight fell on Linnaeus.

René Malaise also had a companion. In the end,

the hermit from the wilderness needed help pulling himself out of the deep borehole of sawfly taxonomy so he could move more freely towards the open spaces of a general synthesis. The companion's name was Nils Odhner, and he was a palaeozoologist, an expert on fossil plankton, a man who didn't make a lot of noise. Malaise, however, did.

Of course, many taxonomists are completely satisfied to sit at their microscopes and fiddle. Mastering something small, whatever it may be, is stimulation enough for them. They leave the world's great riddles to others. Systematizers in particular often know themselves well enough to stick to their lathes, but we need to remember that Malaise worked at a time when buttonologists swung their arms more freely than they do today. Why is a matter for discussion, but I think one of the reasons that rather narrowly specialized entomologists and botanists speculated as freely as they did was that they were involved in natural history in the true sense of the word. What's more, both plant and animal geography – that is, the history of the distribution of flora and fauna – was something of a

Swedish specialty within the biological sciences. One of the leaders in this area was Eric Hultén. Based on his Kamchatka experience and on other, later travels, he had built a respected position in the sensitive debate about which areas of the globe had been covered by ice during the most recent period of glaciation. Similarly, beetle expert Carl H. Lindroth had been able to make important contributions to the more distant history of the northern hemisphere.

So Malaise was only one in a line of biologists who read nature's footnotes as a key to the great riddles. And naturally he chose one of the greatest – Atlantis, the island that sank into the sea. It was no myth. He had proof. In the mid-30s at the latest, perhaps earlier, he got on to the track of the solution, and he never gave up. The last pamphlet he wrote on the question – 'Atlantis, a verified myth' – came out as late as 1973, when he was more than eighty years old. But by then no one was listening.

The background to this obsession is that our friend Malaise, now a global authority on sawflies, had begun to ponder the fact that someone in Patagonia, of all places, had caught a sawfly whose closest relatives were found in Europe. It was a classic zoogeographic problem, a mystery of the kind that scientists had previously tried to solve with the help of various hypothetical land bridges between the continents but that since the 1940s they increasingly tended to explain with the theory of continental drift. This is the one we believe in today – the idea that the continents were once clumped together in a single land mass, Pangaea, that later broke into several parts, roughly the way an ice floe breaks up in the spring. If only the animals or plants were sufficiently ancient, continental drift could explain even the strangest dispersions.

Like Gregor Mandel's discoveries about the labyrinthine ways of heredity, the theory about the continents' journey across the globe had lain on the table for a long time before acquiring any consequence. Its originator, the German geophysicist Alfred Wegener (1880–1930), was not, of course, the first person to notice that Africa's west coast and South America's east coast fit together like pieces in a puzzle, but it was he who first formulated the theory that they had actually once been joined. That was in 1912. But since he could not explain where the force that moved the continents came from, hardly anyone paid him any attention. It was only several decades later that more and more scientists began to take his theory seriously. Biologists in particular liked the idea, while geologists remained doubtful for some time. The real breakthrough came only in the 1960s.

When, after many years of hard work, Malaise finally presented and published his doctoral dissertation on Asian sawflies – the year was 1945 – biologists had begun getting used to the notion that all the world's continents came from a single ancient land mass. But not Malaise. For him, Wegener's theory was humbug. The earth's crust, he insisted, was far too thick. No force on earth could be strong enough to propel such a sideways migration. Never. He found particularly ridiculous that piece of the theory that said the Indian subcontinent had come whizzing along from the south with such force that the collision with the rest of Asia had pushed up the Himalayas and the Tibetan plateau. Not a chance. And so it came about that this apparently narrow dissertation about hymenoptera in faraway places grew into a frontal attack on a theory that had a real future. When you read his book, which is no easy task, you get the impression that sawfly research was something of a capacious booster rocket beneath a warhead of pure geology, targeted on the new creation narrative.

Wegener was wrong. Nils Odhner was right.

And what was Odhner's theory?

Before we go into that, we need to observe that at about this time Malaise became involved in a protracted, implacable conflict with his boss in the entomological department, Professor Olof Lundblad. The origin of the feud is shrouded in darkness, but the archive of the Royal Swedish Academy of Sciences contains an impressive bundle of written complaints about purely trivial matters, indicating that the conflict quite quickly became one of those pianos that play themselves. For example, neither one of them hesitated to turn to the highest authority in a dispute about how many minutes Malaise was allowed to take for his daily lunch. My guess is that Lundblad simply got sick and tired of the no doubt insufferably independent Malaise, especially since he spent more and more time with Odhner in the palaeozoological department, deep into speculations about matters that by no means fell within his professional purview.

There's a story still told today about how Malaise came sauntering in after lunch one afternoon, unquestionably late, and there by the lift stood Lundblad in a rage, staring pointedly at his wristwatch. Whereupon Malaise remarked, casually, 'Timing an egg?'

Anyway, Odhner had worked out a whole theory of his own about how the earth came to look the way it does. This intellectual construct, which came to be called the constriction theory, was, if we're to believe Malaise, ingenious in its simplicity. And it explained everything. In rough outline, constriction theory maintains that high mountains and deep valleys, both on land and under the seas, are created when the planet's skin develops folds under the pressures that arise from differences in temperature, not from mystical currents in the earth's interior. In short, climate, or at least temperature, controls the whole process. It's true that even in Odhner's model, the earth's crust is divided into plates, separated by unstable zones with earthquakes and volcanoes, but in contrast to Wegener's more mobile entities, Odhner's do not move laterally to any marked degree. They just expand or shrink depending on temperature. The continents lie where they lie, and if the climate is warm, the plates expand, whereupon mountain chains crumple upwards and ocean trenches fold down. More or less like corrugated sheet-metal.

I'm reluctant to go into all of this in greater depth. Constriction theory is not exactly crystal clear, and my knowledge of geology is not striking. On top of which I don't think we need to know so much more than that – from this moment on – René Malaise was fully invested in an idea that almost no one else took seriously. The sawflies had been nothing but a conveyance. Now he had arrived. That he would soon land out in the cold was something understood by everyone but Malaise himself.

He made a great mistake. Instead of using Odhner's theory as a resource in addressing his zoogeographic questions, which would have been an honourable position in other people's eyes, he dropped the sawflies abruptly and threw himself head first into the tangle of legends and essentially fruitless speculation that begins with Plato's story of the sunken Atlantis. His enthusiasm was as boundless as always. He seems to have been utterly unaffected by the laughter behind his back. For all I know, he was remembering his trap. That too had been dismissed as wishful thinking. But perseverance carried the day that time. Why not now again? Although what's more likely is that he didn't think about it at all, at least not about what other people thought. He had endured inhospitable climates before. Loneliness too, for that matter.

With his popularly written book *Atlantis, a Geological Reality*, which appeared in Swedish in 1951, Malaise burned his last bridge to serious science. The situation could still have been rescued, and his reputation saved for posterity, if he had only restrained himself a bit. Odhner's ideas about plate tectonics were a theory as good as any other, and its originator possessed impressive knowledge about the dispersion of the planet's fauna. A sunken continent in the Atlantic, perhaps at about the latitude of the Azores, was not such a big deal. It was a wild hypothesis, of course, but still only a hypothesis, supported by facts from solid research in many disciplines. He might have got away with it.

But no. Why limit yourself?

Sometimes I think it was his experiences as a young man that led him astray. The memory of earthquakes and devastating tsunamis. There was probably no other scientist on earth who had felt the power released when the sea bottom suddenly falls several hundred metres – not the way he had, in his very bones. A hundred thousand people had died in the Japanese catastrophe in 1923. He was there.

> The catastrophe that legend tells us did away with Atlantis could very well have had its equivalent in reality. The principal settlement could have experienced a sudden drop with subsequent flooding, caused by an abrupt settling of the bedrock as the result of marginal constriction. We have examples from Japan of the way large areas have suddenly sunk in

connection with an earthquake. As noted earlier,
parts of Sagami Bay outside Tokyo sank by as much
as 400 metres. If the narrow, culture-bearing coastal
belt with its principal settlements was subjected to
this kind of widespread destruction, it could very well
have meant ruin for the entire nation and its culture.
The tsunami waves that followed in the wake of the
disaster could have contributed to the elimination of
the coastal populations. Once the coastal inhabitants
and cultural centres were gone, the remaining people
may have emigrated or gradually gone under.

So ends the final chapter of the Atlantis book of 1951. It is not long, just ten pages, but long enough to upset the entire apple cart. The chapter's title is 'Atlantis's significance for human culture'. The man holding the pen does not say in so many words that human beings lived on Atlantis, nor that they had contact with the Egyptians, nor that they were the globe's most daring and powerful seafarers. Not explicitly. And he does not say that he knows for certain that these Atlanteans built Stonehenge in England, nor that they provided all the bronze we find in the earth from our own bronze age, nor that it is their ships we find depicted on innumerable Swedish rock carvings from the same period.

And yet the whole book radiates a belief that these things are true.

A long time later, in 1969, the book came out in English, now under the trickier title *A New Deal in Geography, Geology and Related Sciences*. He had to publish it at his own expense. Much had happened during those years. The continental drift theory had emerged victorious, Odhner was more anonymous than ever, and Malaise himself must have seemed a living fossil. Fifty years had passed since he went to Kamchatka. Who had ever heard of that expedition? Maybe it's not so strange that, in the English edition, the chapter about the culture of Atlantis had grown to almost sixty pages.

Atlantis was now the cradle of human culture, the very pulsing heart of a vanished golden age. Reading it today, I find it all touching and rather exhilarating. After all, René is my friend. That his narrative can be seen as a treasure trove for New Age fantasists doesn't bother me in the least.

On the other hand, I was particularly struck by something he wrote in his preface. It gave me an idea.

> Scientists of to-day, be it geologists, geophysicists, or oceanographers, are so overspecialized that they master only a limited sector of their own branch. Outside this sector they hardly dare to express an opinion. The fundamental theories on which, for instance, geology is based have mostly been in use for generations and have in their mind ceased to be theories and have attained almost the standing of axioms.

. . .

I managed with some difficulty to get my hands on a copy of this book about Atlantis, and the same day it arrived in the mail I sent it off to a geologist I know who lives in Madrid and whose expertise I trust – ever since we crossed the Ural Mountains together. That was towards the end of the 1980s. We were on our way to a large gas field on the Yamal Peninsula in northern Siberia for reasons that were anything but clear, and we were taking the train east from Moscow with some energetic Russians. We sat up all night drinking and singing the way you do in Russian train compartments, and when morning dawned without our even having noticed our passage through the mountains, my friend the geologist said, 'I wonder if maybe the Urals are a fraud.'

Of even greater importance for his credibility and temperament is the fact that he has been working in the oil industry for a long time. Self-interest doesn't lie. Academic prestige and sloppy thinking vanish quickly in a world where a single wrong guess about where the oil is can cost hundreds of millions. Now I was asking him to comment on Malaise and the long-forgotten constriction theory.

Weeks passed, and then came a long letter, written in Hassi Messaoud, a remote hole in eastern Algeria where my friend was stationed for the moment in order to assess an especially promising oil field.

Because he lived and worked in French-speaking

countries for many years, he began by lamenting Malaise's unfortunate name (which can refer to everything from nausea to economic difficulties) but quickly moved on to some informal reflections on the various theories about the earth's history. Very true, he wrote, Wegener's good old continental drift should be considered axiomatic. Everyone buys it. The theory now explains everything in geology – lock, stock and barrel. We can even measure the speed of the drift. My friend wrote that Europe and North America are gliding apart about as rapidly as fingernails grow. That is to say, about two centimetres a year. Although on the other hand, he added, it is impossible to determine whether these measurements are accurate.

The same is true of the theory as a whole. It's not possible to say definitively that it describes reality, only that it fits well enough with what we can observe. But to dismiss it as false is even less plausible. 'With its help we find oil again and again, but despite that, we probably can't exclude the possibility that it contains defects, or that one day it won't have to be discarded.'

Who knows? When everything is said and done,

the days of really revolutionary breakthroughs are perhaps not over. Maybe, sooner or later, someone will sweep Wegener right out of the door. Let's keep our fingers crossed, for the sake of René, my friend.

Chapter 15

The Legible Landscape

They say you can't be a really good geologist without an exceptional feeling for time. A feeling, not knowledge. Empirical knowledge is different; it's a thing you can acquire with hard work and patient effort. But a feeling for time is inborn, an aptitude, like musicality, that can only rarely be developed from scratch, and it is said to be the secret behind the very best geologists. I don't know if this is true. But it makes sense.

For what is ten thousand years, actually? Or three million? In relation to a billion? The rest of us have no idea. We can understand the figures, like lines on a scale, and it may be that we can to some extent grasp the metaphor in which the history of the earth is represented as an hour, while humanity's time on its surface is reckoned only in seconds. But our feeling for temporal space is absent.

My own grasp of temporal spaces so great that they border on eternity is always dependent on that kind of mental prosthesis – clumsy synthetic rulers as a substitute for the deeper understanding I lack. Even the time stretching out beyond the lives of people now living can be hard to get a grip on except as numbers and anecdotes. An inborn feeling for time is presumably the same gift that makes a really good evolutionary biologist or any other kind of historian. I sometimes wish I were one of them, and I have tried, but my downfall is always precisely that sense of time. A couple of hundred years, fine, but then the exhaustion of insufficiency comes creeping in.

That's why I go collecting with my net in the here and now and read my landscape in the present tense. Believe me, even that narrative is rich and full of surprises, however near-sighted you happen to be.

When you get right down to it, my whole history

with hoverflies is also a question of comprehension – we might call it language-oriented. Why flies? I realize that I haven't been entirely honest in describing my motives. I've answered the question badly. I was so full of my determination not to lie about some hypothetical benefit that I presented my proclivity for catching flies as a matter of cheap anaesthesia and the simple pleasures of the hunt, an outlet for the vanity of a poor man and the eternal longing to be best. And that may be true, but there is something else too, maybe not greater but anyway prettier. More honourable. It shouldn't be so – an ambitious person's path to the perfection of God-knows-what should be worthy of all honour, if only because a world full of highly personal mastery without petty rivalry would be a nice place to live.

In any case, learning a language is never wrong.

So for a moment let us consider the ability to read the landscape as if it were a language, how to understand nature almost as if it were literature, experience it in the same way that we experience art or music. It's all a question of landscape literacy. Now you may object that all of us, regardless of education and custom, can appreciate beauty in various works of art and pieces of music. That's true. But it's equally true that the untrained sensibility is easily captivated by what is sweetly charming and romantic, which can of course be good but which is nevertheless only a first impression and does not lead very far. Art has a language to be learned; music too has hidden subtleties.

The necessary conditions are more distinct in literature. If you can't read, you can't read. And when I say that the landscape can provide a kind of literary experience at different depths I mean just exactly that – to begin with, you have to know the language. In a vocabulary of nothing but animals and plants, the flies can thus be seen as glosses, telling stories of every kind within the framework of the grammatical laws set down by evolution and ecology.

To recognize a *Chrysotoxum vernale* when you see it, to know why it's flying in just this place and at just this moment, is a source of satisfaction not all that easy to account for. I'm afraid that our path to what is beautiful must first pass through what is meaningful. Which is the more important will remain a matter of taste.

Chrysotoxum vernale is very handsome and, in the manner of hoverflies, it looks like a wasp. Anyone who can see the difference can already read, but it gets really exciting only when you can distinguish it from *Chrysotoxum arcuatum*. And by my soul, that's not easy. In years of training, you have to catch both of the twins and examine them on pins, because what is decisive in identifying the species is primarily the colour of the inner quarter of the front legs.

Therefore I have collected several specimens over the years. In fact, I have fussed with the *Chrysotoxum* to such an extent that I believe I can tell them apart in the field without even having to catch them in my net. And so I know that *arcuatum* is common, while *vernale* is a rarity. And why is that the case? The question is as open as a half-read novel.

My collection contains six *vernale* from the island, collected in different years between 27 May and 19 June. Clearly their fly time is that brief. That's interesting. Even more interesting is the fact that aside from these six flies, this species is known in modern central Sweden from a single specimen – from another island a few minutes of latitude south of mine. The fly is abundant on the islands of Öland and Gotland and in Skåne as well, but it is otherwise absent from the mainland. In the nineteenth century it was collected in Blekinge and Småland, Östergötland and Västergötland, but no longer. Why?

Our knowledge is never adequate, but we know enough to formulate at least a respectably supportable hypothesis. Nothing is more useful than a hypothesis. Particularly because now and then the collector is forced to endure conversations with uncultured individuals who think they know that anyone who would hurt a fly must be immoral and a brute. They're of the ecological persuasion, if I may be pardoned the expression – gentle flagellants who hunker down beside their ill-smelling compost piles and rest easy in the certainty that much of life on earth has run its course. They are severely tormented by nightmares of extermination. You can see it in their eyes.

And so a hypothesis can cheer them up. And *Chrysotoxum vernale* is a good candidate.

With all the rhetorical cunning I can muster, I

would like to turn off into a byway and say something partly irrelevant about how Linnaeus was gripped by such wonder and awe in the face of nature's riches when he saw our most beautiful butterfly that he christened it *Parnassius apollo*. Everyone recognizes an Apollo butterfly. In a picture, I mean, because in the real world there are fewer and fewer people granted the gift of watching its fumbling flight across marshy meadows and bare granite. On the mainland, the Apollo has disappeared from most of the provinces where it once flew, and now in these ultimate days it is common only here and along the southeast coast. Something has happened over the last half century. We don't know what, but scientists are investigating and thinking more and more audibly that the land itself is sick where the Apollo used to fly. Increased acidity is thought to leach out elements in the soil that get into the plants and then wind up . . . well, they don't really know, but they guess there's a connection.

That the Apollo butterfly still exists here on the island is said to depend on the fact that the bedrock is limestone, which gives the soil the capacity to withstand the poisons and pollution of our industrial society. This is in any case one hypothesis, and it can be transferred word for word to the hoverfly *Chrysotoxum vernale*.

The sceptic feels a bit better at once, partly because he always glows slightly in the cosy darkness of approaching apocalypse, partly because he believes he's speaking to an idealist, a barefoot scientist who has dedicated his life to the heroic task of mapping the evil of the age by searching for flies that will soon be extinct. Suddenly my hunt is pleasing in the eyes of God, almost a praiseworthy testimonial, and that is not a bad description, but to present this empirically cool, scientific usefulness as my primary motive would be simply ridiculous and the height of hypocrisy. That reading is only self-important.

No one learns to tell the song of the woodlark from that of the skylark in order to make it easier to detect approaching catastrophe. All of that comes later. The flies are just smaller and more numerous. The motive is the same, and the reward. Dare I mention beauty?

When the woodlark comes from the south in

March, something happens to those who recognize its song. Something happens to everyone else too, of course, for birdsong is always birdsong, but soon the whole forest is full of robins, hedge warblers, song thrushes, greenfinches, tree creepers and wrens, all of them singing for all they're worth, and that does dilute that delicate joy. It's only when you can tell them apart and know their names that you can read on and finally understand. The more glosses you know, the richer the experience becomes. Like reading a book. It's rarely the important books that give the greatest reading pleasure.

Television has taught us to see nature like a film, as something immediately comprehensible and available, but that is only an illusion. The narrative voice-over is missing when you go outdoors. What seems great art and sweet music on the surface becomes, for the uninitiated, an impenetrable body of text in a foreign language. So the best answer to the question of why I collect hoverflies is, ultimately, that I want to understand the fine print in the only language that's been mine for as long as I can remember.

In high summer, in July, when all the summer

people are lying like seals on the outermost skerries, I often retreat to a remote place on the southern part of the island to read the landscape. On a gentle slope at the edge of a wood, between a hayfield and an avenue of high-voltage towers, there is a large stand of broad-leaved sermountain growing among the oaks and hazels, which, when the sun is at its zenith, attracts fantastic hordes of insects to its large, white umbels. I usually see the noble chafer there, *Gnorimus nobilis*, and out on the hayfield, without a care in the world, are Burnet moths, to whose odd colour only Harry Martinson gives full justice: 'The prime colour of the wing is a dark, inky, blue-green blue; carmine-red spots shimmer against that background.'

On that slope, every summer, I also see the puzzling bee fly *Villa paniscus*, a darting tuft of wool that no one knows anything about and that was thought to be extinct until last year, mostly because few if any people could tell it from *Villa hottentotta* (yes, that's really its name). Bee flies are really for extra credit, but there's something about that slope that attracts me for the sake of reading something other than hoverflies. *Anthrax leucogaster* is also found there, another relatively un-known bee fly, and my latest find was the gold wasp *Chrysis hirsuta*, which is of no interest to anyone, but I wanted to mention it all the same. Partly because there's no risk involved, I mean, no one can suspect me of us-ing my knowledge of some expert's unknown opus to make myself look good, partly because my whole point is that reading nature is a bottomless activity.

I could probably spend a whole life down there (winter doesn't count) without ever getting the feeling that I've now read everything. The hoverflies alone, my personal footnotes, would keep me adequately occupied. For example, the broad-leaved sermountain flowers are often visited by both of the imposing spe-cies in the genus *Spilomyia* – not every day, of course, for these are legendary creatures with the power to make environment bureaucrats jump up and down with excitement, that's how rare they are. And the story they tell with their very presence is rich in old, rotting, protection-worthy trees. My heart raced the first time, so great was my eagerness to capture, own, learn and boast with a *Spilomyia*, and nowadays the feeling is somehow even greater, now when I see them again – and read. Like the woodlark in March. Might I call it joy?

There are other stories that you have to write yourself. Like the one about *Eumerus grandis*.

It takes place one storey down, closer to the ground. Hoverflies of the genus *Eumerus* develop precisely the same way as the closely related narcissus fly, in various kinds of plant roots, but for some reason they've never been big on visiting flowers. In fact it was several years before I discovered them, because I was so concentrated on studying what was going on in the sermountain's blossoms. There were actually several different species flying around down there in the undergrowth, and one of them turned out to be *grandis*. Host plant unknown. So said the literature. I was in no hurry.

It's important to the story that *Eumerus grandis* is one of those mysterious flies that are found all across Europe but that are common nowhere, at least not so far as we know. Maybe it occurs in numbers here and there where no one sees it. So long as the host plant is unknown, we don't know where to look. Or to be exact, so long as the host plant *was* unknown. It is no longer. It is known to me. One day as I sat there in the grass, I caught sight of a female acting suspiciously down near the base of a withered sermountain in a crack in the rock. She was running around in circles on the ground, more or less like a chicken with its head cut off. She kept it up for half an hour before she flew away, whereupon I examined the leaves she'd been running on through my loupe – and found eggs so small they were almost invisible.

This was the forefront of scientific research in ultra-fine print. A discovery! I began reading the landscape more avidly and have since found the fly in other places where broad-leaved sermountain grows. I know this creature, perhaps better than anyone else in the whole world. I ought to write a scientific paper about it in some specialized journal, but that hasn't happened. Still, rumours spread pretty fast anyway, among the experts.

Chapter 16

Doctor Orlík and I

To be on the safe side, I have got myself a guardian angel. Doctor Orlík. Since he's immortal, and only a peripheral figure, I figure he has time to watch over my destiny if anyone does. He knows what it's about.

> *'Dragonflies?' Orlík frowned. 'I have not interest. I have only interest for Musca domestica.'*
>
>   *'The common house-fly?'*
>
>   *'That is what it is.'*
>
>   *'Answer me,' Utz interrupted again. 'On which day did God create the fly? Day Five? Or Day Six?'*

> '*How many times will I tell you?*' Orlík clam-
> oured. '*We have one hundred ninety million years of
> flies. But you will always speak of days!*'
> '*Hard words,*' said Utz, philosophically.

Yes, it's there we find him, in Bruce Chatwin's short
novel *Utz*, his best book and the last one he wrote before death took him in January 1989. The first-person
narrator recalls a trip to Prague in the summer of 1967,
the year before the Russian tanks, when a magazine ed-
itor assigned him to write an article about Rudolf II's
attempt to cure his depression by collecting exotic objects. His idea at the time was that the article would
be included in a larger work about the psychopatho-
logy of the manic collector, but as a result of linguistic
confusion and laziness, he says, the Czech expedition
was a failure, not much more than a pleasant holiday at
someone else's expense.

Only when his life is almost over, more than twenty
years later, does it bear fruit.

But back to Prague.

The narrator has a good friend who is a specialist on

the lands behind the Iron Curtain, and this man advises him to look up Kaspar Utz, an eccentric gentleman who, when he was still a child, found his calling as a collector of Meissen porcelain. Utz is a genuine oddball who now owns more than a thousand figurines, worth a fortune, and has cleverly squired them unscathed through the world war as well as Stalin's persecutions. They meet at the Restaurant Pstruh, where it turns out that Utz has eaten lunch with his good friend Doctor Orlík every Thursday since 1946. Now they sit waiting for the doctor to arrive, and Utz tells him that Orlík is a famous scientist, a specialist in the parasites of the woolly mammoth but also a well-known expert on flies.

We did not have to wait long before a gaunt, bearded figure in a shiny double-breasted suit pushed its way through the revolving doors.

This unforgettable meal in the heart of Prague threatens constantly to go off the rails because of the unpredictable Doctor Orlík. It begins with the three men at the table all deciding to order carp, which, incidentally, is the only thing the restaurant has to offer that day. In the process, the narrator discovers that a mistake has been made in translating the multi-language menu. The English word *carp* has been confused with *crap*, which he is thoughtless enough to point out.

> *'In England,' I said, 'this fish is called "carp".*
> *"Crap" has a different meaning.'*
> > *'Oh?' said Dr Orlík. 'What meaning?'*
> > *'Faeces,' I said. 'Shit.'*

Orlík finds this hugely amusing. Dishes such as *Crap soup with paprika*, *Fried crap* and *Crap balls* immediately become wonderful jokes that make him writhe with laughter, not to mention *Crap à la juive*, 'Shit in the Jewish manner', which he promptly insists on ordering in order to tease his Jewish friend Utz.

> *'And to begin,' asked the waiter.*
> > *'Nothing,' said Orlík. 'Only the crap!'*

The narrator, who is afraid that Utz will soon have had enough and just get up and leave, takes evasive action.

> *I tried to swing the conversation to Utz's collection of porcelain. His reaction was to swivel his neck inside his collar and say, blankly, 'Dr Orlík is also a collector. But he is a collector of flies.'*
>
> *'Flies?'*
>
> *'Flies,' assented Orlík.*

It is here that the narrator brings up the dragonflies. Englishmen are exceptionally gifted conversationalists in tight situations, and he now recalls some particularly beautiful dragonflies he had seen on a trip to Brazil. As noted earlier, however, Orlík is not interested in anything but houseflies, so he continues to tease Utz, among other things by criticizing Franz Kafka for his questionable presentation of the insect in his short story 'Metamorphosis'. The lunch is indeed unforgettable.

But let us leave the squabbling gentlemen at Restaurant Pstruh for a moment in order to have a brief but closer look at how I happen to have chosen as my guardian angel a man who shows such a pronounced disdain for every fly but the housefly. The fact is that his lack of interest, I am convinced, was only an unfortunate symptom of popular opinion at the time. Today, after the boom, he would have answered differently, I am certain of that. I know his type.

So I must say something about the 'hoverfly boom'. I hear the expression from time to time among entomologists.

'So I see you've been drawn into this hoverfly boom.'

What these surprising words mean is that more than five people in Sweden have begun to take an interest in hoverflies in recent years. Everything is relative. But the fact is that something is happening that no one could have suspected until quite recently. Among nature's innumerable annotations, hoverflies, the family Syrphidae, have risen up to tell an especially tempting and promising fund of useful and entertaining stories. For too long, the small change of environmental politics has been lichens, mushrooms and other humble tokens of the wilderness. But fashions change here too, and the time has now come to use the colourful yardstick of the hoverflies to measure the value of the natural world we have to some extent created.

This is an obvious idea and a good one. Partly because hoverflies tell us so very much about the landscape, inasmuch as the demands of the different species are so varied and particular. Partly because this information is readily available thanks to the fact that the creatures are relatively easy to recognize. They sit there right before our eyes, everywhere, in flowers and on sunlit leaves (when they're sheltered from the wind). There are neither too many species nor too few. They are neither too familiar nor too exotic. In other words, everything about them is just right. People who study, say, dragonflies or butterflies quickly get to know all the different kinds, even if they have a whole country to work with. They know how they live and where they're found and, worst of all, they soon find themselves with the saddest of all collections – one that's complete.

Moreover, many hoverflies are good indicators of environments that today's Europeans passionately seek out and protect – marshes, meadows, virgin forests, parks.

In short, the hoverfly boom is a European phenomenon. Lively activity has broken out in many European countries, among both scientists and amateurs. Over the course of just a few years, hoverflies have become so popular as objects of research that they compete for attention with pretty much any other insect. Maybe I'm biased, but sometimes I get the impression that not even the butterfly nuts will maintain their historically solid lead. Belgians, Brits, Danes, Germans, Spaniards, Dutchmen, Russians, Czechs and Norwegians – they all seem to be running themselves ragged after hoverflies.

The background is in some sense language-based. The appearance of a marvellous book, *De sweefvliegen van Noordwest-Europa en Europees Rusland, in het bijzonder van de Benelux*, published in Amsterdam in 1981, introduced a trend that resulted in a whole series of splendid field guides to European hoverflies. The English and the Danes did the most to literally translate hoverflies and make them readable, but the Belgians, Russians and

Germans also produced very useful, modern guides. So the way was paved.

Over the course of just a few years, hoverflies became accessible even for amateur collectors, and it wasn't long before hoverfly literature broke through on all fronts. Titles like *Dorset Hoverflies* and *Somerset Hoverflies* began to appear in England, a kind of local guide full of species lists and range maps where each find of even the tiniest fly was marked with a black dot. The Germans, always one step behind, but on the other hand more thorough, responded with *Untersuchung zum Vorkommen der Schwebfliegen in Niedersachsen und Bremen*, more than 500 pages thick. And so it's gone. My favourite in the genre is *Hoverflies of Surrey*, in part because the pictures are so pretty, in part because they have found just as many species – 202 – as I have found on the island. Surrey covers an area of 1,679 square kilometres. My island measures fifteen, as I mentioned earlier.

One day, I think, I'm going to write one of those local field guides. In English. Just to show off. No other reason.

Anyway, the identification guides set off the boom, and now everything is moving along under its own power. Every issue of the German journal *Volucella*, which deals exclusively with hoverflies, contains a special section with the title 'Neue Schwebfliegen-Literatur' ('New Hoverfly Publications'). In the latest issue, which is 260 pages thick, this new publication section catalogues more than 400 titles. And the next couple of years will see the first Swedish guide since 1909. A doorstop, a magnificent book with every species portrayed in scrupulous detail in newly painted water-colours, written by my friend the foremost expert, the man who once introduced me to hoverfly high society.

Needless to say, Doctor Orlík would have been interested in hoverflies if *Utz* had been written a few years later. Take my word for it.

But that's not important. There's another side of Orlík that both attracts and frightens me, as is so often the case with guardian angels. He really knows how to limit himself. I mean, he studies only one species of fly. But at the same time, there's something superficial about him, and vacillating, as if at any moment he was about to run away. Chatwin knew what he was doing when he created this man.

And yet Chatwin himself was not much of an entomologist, although it's said that he collected butterflies once when he was fifteen years old and spent a couple of months on Lundby Farm by Lake Yngaren in Södermanland. Much has been written about Bruce Chatwin's travels around the world, but this, his first trip abroad, in the summer of 1955, remains a footnote.

The farm was owned by the once famous doctor Ivan Bratt – the man who invented Sweden's version of alcohol rationing in 1917 – and the idea was that during his stay in Sweden, Bruce would teach a bit of the noble art of English conversation to two of Bratt's grandsons, Thomas and Peter. But little came of it. The boys thought Bruce was odd and undeserving of anything but nettles in his bed and other forms of bullying, so he hunted butterflies instead. And spent time with the boys' uncle Percival, who lived on the farm, an elderly eccentric who in his youth had abandoned everything and tried to treat a deep depression by retreating to the

Sahara Desert. In his old age, he still kept a small chest of sand from that journey.

When he visited Peter Bratt in Stockholm shortly before his death, Chatwin said it was during his meetings with Percival that summer in Södermanland that he decided what he wanted to do with his life. What became of the butterfly collection is not known. Presumably it was thrown out and is gone for good.

. . .

Doctor Orlík, too, had other interests. *Utz* is a rather complex novel for all its simplicity. The narrator tries to maintain contact with the bizarre Meissen collector, but the connection is broken after the Soviet occupation. Orlík, on the other hand, continues to write. In a stream of letters in his illegible scrawl, he honours his English acquaintance with pleas for expensive books and photocopies of scientific articles, begs money, asks for forty pairs of socks or orders his correspondent to track down some odd woolly mammoth bones in the Natural History Museum.

*One letter informed me of his current project: a study of the house-fly (*Musca domestica*), as painted in Dutch and Flemish still-lifes of the seventeenth century. My role in this enterprise was to examine every photograph of paintings by Bosschaert, Van Huysum or Van Kessel, and check whether or not there was a fly in them.*

I did not reply.

This correspondence too dries up, but many years later, when the narrator happens to pass through Prague, he decides to track down Utz's long-since-vanished porcelain collection. In the palaeontological department of the National Museum he finds the now retired Doctor Orlík busy cleaning the shinbone of a mammoth. Together they make their way once again to Restaurant Pstruh.

'How are the flies?' I asked.

'I have returned to the mammoth.'

'I mean your collection of flies.'

'I have thrown.'

Chapter 17

The Allotted Time

The children were swimming down by the jetty, the sun was hot, everyone was in the water except me, sitting in the shade with my back against the wall. All I could manage was to read the paper, only the shortest items, meaningless summer news stories, of which one of thirteen lines informed me that a group of scientists in Australia had succeeded in figuring out how many stars there are in the universe. To be more exact, it seems there are ten times as many stars as there are grains of sand on earth.

On all the beaches, in all the deserts, everywhere.

This cheered me up at once and I forgot the heat.

I travelled across the Sahara once, from Ouargla to Agadez, so I understand very well the scope of the astronomers' discovery. Just estimating the total number of sand grains can be considered something of an achievement. But it was not this that cooled me and made me so happy, not the counting itself, but rather the fresh and nearly idiotic optimism of their attempt to explain. They didn't say that the stars are incomprehensibly numerous, which would have been correct but still only a lifeless fact. They gave a number. With more zeros than you can count. Explaining the comprehensible is no challenge. But this!

True, the item ended somewhat timidly by saying that the estimate was valid only for that part of the universe that could be seen with a telescope, but by the time I'd read that far my failing will to live had already been restored. And when a certain Dr Simon Driver on the next to last line extended the accumulating indecisiveness by remarking that the number of stars might also be infinite, I was already on my way. Nothing, and I do mean nothing, stimulates my imagination like this kind of utterly ineffective effort to describe something, the dumber the better.

Against all odds, some poor presbyopic chump takes a shot at it, maybe so he won't make himself ill by sensing a truth no one else sees. And he falls flat on his face, of course, his truth as incomprehensible and strange as it was to begin with. But at least he's tried.

And I thought, if someone can cheer me up this much by completely failing to describe a thing that doesn't even interest me, then the last barrier has fallen. Nothing can stop me now. In his metaphor about the stars and the grains of sand, Dr Driver had set the bar quite wonderfully low. Now everything was possible. At one blow, the heat had lost its power over my senses. I stood up and went into the library, closed the door, sat down at my desk, pulled out the telephone jack. Closed my eyes.

I had always imagined that this story would be quick to tell.

That isn't the way it's turned out.

No, nothing's turned out the way I imagined. This simple history that interests no one turned out to be inhabited by a person named René Malaise, a madman who invented a trap and then went off the tracks, a man forgotten for good reason. What was he doing in here? Was it just my old attraction to losers? Or was it simply that Malaise – the prolific Malaise, the man who truly never limited himself – reminded me that concentration is always greatest when there is no rear exit? When time is measured, and maybe space?

Someone had told me about his death. A banal anecdote, one of many, but for me of course it was more important than all the others. It reminded me of travel, my own youthful travels. Because we all go off on long journeys that turn out to be full of disappointments. It is only much later that the earthquakes or other experiences, whatever they may have been, acquire significance.

Malaise grew old the way entomologists do. Ebba had been dead for several years, and he lived by himself on memories and fish. Until well into November, he usually stayed alone in Simpnäs, up in Roslagen, mostly for the sake of the fishing and fighting with his neighbours, but since he already had four heart attacks behind him, his doctors tried to get him to take it a little easier that last summer. Lay four nets, they said, not eight. He laid twelve – of course. There had been a strong wind that day at the end of June 1978, so his nets had picked up a lot of seaweed. Just pulling them out of the water was a tough job, but he wouldn't give up. He wasn't the type. It was only when he was back at his leaky house, beating the seaweed out of his twelve nets, that he had the final heart attack.

He managed to call the helicopter ambulance himself, and he was conscious the whole way in to Danderyd Hospital, where he died.

Malaise was a good storyteller. Everyone agrees on that. And he was one hell of a traveller. But that last journey, as it's been related to me, was a confirmation of something else as well. Of what can happen when time is short and you know it. For it's said that he lay at the front of the helicopter's glass bubble, dying, and talked with beaming delight and almost lyrical euphoria about all the islands they passed, down there beneath them in the glittering sea. It was all over and he knew it. I want to believe that he was satisfied.

. . .

Not four years later, in March 1982, I sat on a black plastic sofa one whole night waiting for a flight at Los Angeles International Airport. After thirteen months of travels around the world, I was now finally on my way home, tired and disillusioned. Miserable. Of course I would keep up appearances – later. It wouldn't be hard, because if you traced my route on a map with your finger, my trip was impressive. But deep down, I never understood what it meant. Except right then, that night.

I had flown in from Tahiti and was waiting for a flight to London. Then home by train and boat. But my plane didn't leave for ten hours. I wasn't particularly sleepy.

For some reason, there weren't many people in the transit hall that night, but right across from me, on a similar sofa, on the other side of a low table, sat a woman of my own age, reading a book by Eduardo

Galeano. We started talking, the way you do in airports at night. She was from Chile. Now she was on her way home to Santiago from Hawaii, where, if I remember right, she had taken part in a course at the university. She too was looking at a ten-hour wait. There were only a few minutes between her departure and mine. Neither of us would be left behind. We would never see one another again. We started talking.

Twenty hours. Ten of hers and ten of mine. Like being in a glass bubble.

Maybe it was merely exhaustion and jet lag that brought out an abnormal honesty. I don't know. Moreover, I was sick, physically run-down as a result of malaria and epidemic hepatitis. I could undoubtedly find other explanations. But my theory, my hypothesis, is that the time itself was like an island and that, as a result, this one night, I understood something about the meaning of travel that I was never able to recapture. I heard myself express it. For years afterwards, I used to visit airports just to talk to people who were about to leave the country – and maybe other things as well – but I never succeeded in recovering the secret.

Few books have captivated me more than *In the Face of Death* by the Swiss jurist Peter Noll (1926–82). He wrote it during his last year of life, when he knew that all would soon be over, and I cannot explain, just state as best I can, how everything has become easier for me since reading it, not because I know something about my allotted time, but rather because the limitations of a quite different kind that I continually search for have . . . Well, I've never been much of a philosopher. Let me just say that limitations cheer me up.

. . .

And, as always when you give up, a tiny rift opens through which the unexpected can force its way precisely because you no longer think you have anything to lose.

On a Friday afternoon in January, in my efforts to learn more about the reportedly very remarkable art collection that René Malaise had surrounded himself with towards the end of his life, I made one last effort with an art historian I'd been in touch with the previous autumn. I had traced the paintings to an air-raid bunker somewhere deep beneath the art department at Umeå University, to which Malaise had donated them in the mid-70s, a few years before he died. The man I was now calling was the only person who was familiar with the paintings in greater detail. He had written about them. Compiled an annotated catalogue. But the manuscript had lain unpublished for years, and in the manner of academics, he was unwilling to let go of the text. Perfectly understandable. My proper upbringing kept me from even pressing him. At that time, back in the autumn, there had been plenty of other threads to untangle.

Now, on the other hand, that art was the last in a series of riddles in the Malaise case. I really needed that catalogue. Moreover, I was following a new lead. There had been a break-in at his villa on Lidingö on 17 July 1978, the day before Malaise's funeral, and the thieves had known exactly what they wanted. The university had not yet collected the paintings, and now five works of art, presumably the most valuable, were gone without a trace. From police archives and people who specialize in stolen art, I had not succeeded in learning much more than that three of the canvases were attributed to Paulus Potter, Jan Polack and Rembrandt van Rijn, and that the investigation had been closed on 15 February 1979. No suspects, no leads, nothing.

But if I could get my hands on photos of the stolen paintings, I thought, I could do some snooping of my own.

The facts in the case are these. Malaise began to take an interest in art as early as the late 1940s. It was a golden age, which art dealers even today have a hard time describing without tears in their eyes. Fabulous quantities of art and antiques circulated during the war, and afterwards, for more or less tragic reasons, a good deal of it found its way to Sweden. Whole boatloads of paintings were shipped here from the east and the south. Absolutely anything might appear on the market.

Over the course of a couple of decades, Malaise bought older European paintings at auctions, flea markets and antique stores, both in Stockholm and in London – that much I knew. I also knew that he bought low and valued high, so high that experts seldom if ever took him seriously. Everyone I spoke to who'd been close to him knew about the art collection, but no one really knew more. Rembrandt was named. Smiles were smiled. The only written testimony I found was a short passage by the American entomologist Robert Leslie Usinger, a world authority on bed bugs and other heteroptera, who, in his memoirs, tells about the International Congress of Entomology in Stockholm City Hall in 1948. He had stayed in the country for several weeks after the meeting in order to study the collections from the frigate *Eugénie*'s trip around the world in the 1850s, which were housed in the Museum of Natural History, and there he had met all the great Swedish experts – Lundblad, Brundin, Bryk, Malaise. And it was clearly the last of these who made the deepest impression. Usinger, who obviously continued his acquaintance with Malaise, concludes his paragraph about the Swedes as follows:

> But the most fascinating thing about Dr Malaise was his hobby of collecting oil paintings of the old masters. His home was filled with the most magnificent paintings, and he showed us his latest collections recently

on our last trip to Stockholm. Dr Malaise claims
that if you know enough and are lucky enough you
can find such paintings in old junk shops and auction
shops, buy them for a modest price, and take them
home and clean them up into such treasures. They are
certainly beautiful, and his home looks like a small
and nicely arranged museum.

So anyway, there I was, resigned and unhappy. It was
Friday. I happened to be in Stockholm and was heading home to the island that evening. The art historian
answered, but he was in a hurry. Asked me to get back
to him later that afternoon. I assumed he just needed
a little time to figure out how to keep me at a distance
and protect his unpublished bunker find. On the other
hand, it was highly probable that the bonanza in the
air-raid shelter was only a collection of forgeries and
clumsy copies, which the easily duped Malaise had
foisted off on the newly opened university in Umeå.

A couple of hours later, I called him back.

Chapter 18

Portrait of Old Man

After that, everything happened very quickly. I suddenly found myself in a kind of mystery play. So let me make use of an unimaginative protocol that builds on dates, names and other details. I need something strict and unimpeachable to reinforce this improbable stew of coincidence.

Three days with my heart in my throat.

When the curtain goes up, I'm on the telephone. It's the afternoon of 23 January 2004. The place is a flat in the Södermalm section of Stockholm, and the art historian I'm talking to is named Hans Dackenberg.

He remembered clearly our conversation of several

months earlier. In fact, my unexpected interest in Malaise had energized him so much that he had immediately resumed work on his catalogue, which was now complete and had been sent to the printer. If I was interested, he could send me a text file at once, all in all about eighty pages, of which one – in reply to my insistent questions – contained a brief list entitled 'Catalogue of works missing from the gift'. The five stolen paintings were indeed by Polack, Potter and Rembrandt – two Rembrandts, not one – plus a painting by Sebastián de Llanos y Valdés, the authenticity of which had once been attested by a certain Sanchez Canton at the Prado Museum in Madrid. Moreover, Dackenberg added, the list included a painting attributed to Michelangelo, which, according to Malaise's own notes, was one of only four known easel paintings by that artist. It was not reported as stolen but was nevertheless missing.

'Are there photographs?'

'No, not of the stolen items.'

I was on the hunt now, for my own sake, and was hoping desperately that the scent would not go cold again. Fortunately, Dackenberg now corrected himself and said that in one case there actually was a photo – the painting by Jan Polack, tempera on a wooden panel, late fifteenth century, depicting Christ with a crystal ball in his hand, had appeared as an illustration for an article by Malaise, published in 1966 in the journal *Samlarnytt* (*Collectors' News*), published by the Collectors Association North Star. The title was 'Yea- or Nay-Sayer'. Dackenberg had included a quotation from it in his catalogue, and he now read it to me over the phone.

> *It is always easier for an art expert to say No instead of Yes and so avoid responsibility for his verdict, especially if no explanation is given. It's the easiest way to hide your own ignorance, although, as the great art expert Max Friedlander says, 'Nay-sayers arouse no credibility unless they occasionally say yes.' Frauds do a lot of damage, of course, but ignorant 'experts' can be just as dangerous for anyone interested in art, though in a different way.*

Collectors' News? I had never heard of this publication. Nor had I ever heard of the Collectors Association

North Star. The phone call came to an end. It was three o'clock. I went out, took the subway to Hötorget and jogged down to Alfa Used Books on Olof Palme Street, where, in a labyrinthine cellar, they store an unfathomable quantity of *periodica*, carefully sorted in brown paper cartons arranged in alphabetical order. Ominously, the clerk had never heard of *Collectors' News* either, but added that if the magazine actually existed anywhere in the world, then the probability was high that it existed here. He gestured in towards the labyrinth and said that I only needed to search alphabetically. I moved into the cellar like a cave diver and went to work.

It did not take me long to find a number of cartons labelled *Collectors' News*. Publication began in 1941, then under the name *Käpphästen* (*Hobby Horse*) and strangely enough it was still being published with an undiminished breadth of subject matter. The magazine dealt with every possible thing that anyone had ever thought of collecting. I now found myself in the wonderful world of the amateur, populated by quirky individuals who collected uniform buttons, corkscrews, cigarette packs, postcards, eggcups, weapons, matchbox labels, dress bayonets, barbed wire, lemon presses, tin soldiers, thimbles, flatirons, player organs, Czechoslovakian razor-blade packages, canes, medals, coins and needles – the works. In one article, a woman wrote proudly about her enormous collection of plastic bags; in another, an elderly gentleman went on about how cool it can be to collect old bandy clubs. Someone else congratulated himself on owning the pope's autograph.

After looking for a while, I found the year I wanted and the issue containing the article about the stolen wood panel. 'By René Malaise, Ph.D.' I glanced through it quickly. Truly a singular story.

Malaise had bought the painting at Bukowski's in 1954. According to the auction catalogue, it was the work of Martin Theophilus Polak, died 1639, which of course our enthusiastic collector doubted. A number of details – among them the gold background, the wood in the panel, and 'the entire type of Christ figure' – indicated instead an earlier artist, probably German. To clear the matter up, he sent a photograph of the painting to the director of the Alte Pinakothek in Munich, Professor Ernst Buchner, who immediately recognized it as an early work of Jan Polack, died 1519. Buchner, who was just then in the process of writing a monograph about Polack, also knew that until the First World War the painting was owned by a certain Frau Barbara Witu in Munich, but from that point on he had, sadly, lost track of it. Malaise, however, could report that it had later appeared in Sweden, first in the collection of one Jaen Jansson, jeweller to the court, and later owned by a wholesaler named Jacobsson, now deceased. His estate had presumably informed the auction house that the painting was by Polack, and the two artists had simply been confused.

Malaise's article now shifted to an attack on ignorant art experts. For example, the curator of the Malmö museum, mercifully not named, turned out to be, freely translated, a feeble-minded, full-blooded fool, who in the early 60s had the bad taste to condemn some of Malaise's Renaissance paintings as forgeries,

> . . . including not only the Jan Polack reproduced above and several other works, but also the painting by Moretto da Brescia which, at the International

Congress in Venice in 1955, I showed to be the
original of Moretto's most distinguished work of art.
The proofs were published in the official deliberations
of the Congress, with illustrations. Following my
lecture, I received two oral assurances that my proofs
were unassailable. I will return to that painting in
a later issue.

Aha! A later issue! I hung up my coat and asked the clerk
if I could borrow a work table. It was after four o'clock.
I started going through the bundles, issue by issue, like
going through the harvest in a Malaise trap in summer.
An hour later, I rushed from the shop to catch the bus
to the evening boat to the island. In my briefcase I had
eleven issues of *Collectors' News* dated from 1961 to 1971,
containing an equal number of contributions from
Malaise, all of them about art except the first, which
was titled 'Collecting Ethnographica in Burma'. I read
all of them, one right after the other, on the road east.

The first one I read was about an oak panel with
a painting of Adam and Eve in Paradise, purchased in
London in 1952, and 'in all probability painted by Jan

Gossart of Maubeuge, called Mabuse (1478?–1533)'. Theory in this case was supported with a lively description of a detailed examination, together with patient study in private and at museums in Germany, Spain and England. Next was a portrait executed by the French court painter Corneille de Lyon, died 1574. Then a large canvas by Alessandro Varotari, called Padovanino (1590–1650), plus, several issues later, the promised exposé of the way Malaise managed to prove to everyone willing to listen that he and he alone owned the preliminary sketch for the six-metre-wide, three-metre-high depiction of Christ in the house of Simon the Pharisee, painted by Moretto da Brescia in the year 1544, which has hung in Chiesa della Pietà in Venice since the middle of the eighteenth century.

I have already mentioned that Malaise went about studying art roughly in the style of an entomologist, some might say a buttonologist. First the hunt in the field, titillating, unpredictable, where plenty of time and sharp senses are the hunter's most powerful tools. Then species identification of the prey, at home at the microscope, in the library, and through comparative studies in museums and private collections. He set to work on his paintings as if they'd been sawflies (or hoverflies), scrutinized the painted figures' knees and the tiniest folds of their bodies, fingers, noses, ears and every other anatomical detail, the smaller the better.

But Malaise discovered that, unfortunately, the other people involved were not entomologists, and in a 1968 article – obviously about the painting ascribed to Michelangelo that subsequently disappeared – he returns to the problem of recalcitrant art experts who insist on saying no. It is money that's taken the fun out of things. The experts simply don't dare to say yes. If they sometimes do so anyway, he snorts, then you can be sure that the expert in question has made certain that he will get a share of the profits. He continues:

Collectors of natural objects are almost always supported by their scientific colleagues, but in the art world, this solidarity seems to be lacking. An incorrect identification of a plant or an insect matters little, but in the art world it can have huge economic consequences and liabilities. A private collector has

*a hard time getting his acquisition acknowledged,
and often this recognition does not come until after
his death, when his collection has passed into public
ownership. At that point, some art historian comes
along and 'discovers' the masterpiece. But the collector can get much pleasure and learn a great deal
by doing his own detective work.*

Say what you like, he never grew bitter. His good
humour seems to have worked like a vaccine against
the kind of distress that so often leads men like Malaise
to a breakdown. Moreover, he unquestionably had
hopes for the future. Sooner or later, some expert
would rediscover his Watteau, for, as I read on the
bus, Ragnar Hoppe at the National Museum had said
that it came from the right period and had the right
coloration, figures, style and conception but was nevertheless not a Watteau, unclear why not. And his two
fifteenth-century works by Andrea Mantegna, one of
them a sketch for a fresco in the Eremitani Chapel in
Padua, what would be their fate? Or the little portrait
of an old man that he ascribed to Frans Hals or possibly

Judith Leyster, which Rembrandt himself had later copied? Maybe the future was his very best friend.

It was pitch black on the jetty, with an ice-cold southwest wind blowing from the bay.

On Saturday I read the catalogue that Dackenberg had sent me on the internet. The gift turned out to consist of thirty works of art, of which five had been stolen and one was simply missing. In addition to those I already knew about, the list included a number of interesting works that contributed to a picture of the collector's taste. Malaise identified a small painting on slate of the Descent from the Cross by Jacopo Bassano (1510–92) as the original for a famous altarpiece (not identified), while he believed that a badly worm-eaten panel – Madonna and Child – was by Pietro Lorenzetti, died about 1348. He attributed a couple of somewhat larger canvases to the Dutchman Aert van de Neer (1603–77) and to the Spanish baroque master Francisco de Zurbarán (1598–1664). A bit unexpectedly, the list also included a couple of nineteenth-century artists, H. C. Bryant and H. W. Hubbard, neither one of whom I'd ever heard of.

The story of how Malaise acquired a landscape of Jan Frans van Bloemen (1662–1749) was rather bewildering. According to his report, the painting was originally purchased directly from the artist, in Rome, by the Russian Czarina Catherine II, whereupon it wound up in the palace of Tsarskoye Selo outside St Petersburg. A long time later, in 1925 to be exact, the revolutionary government decided to weed out the paintings from the royal palaces, and the van Bloemen, in spite of having been selected by the Hermitage Museum, was for some odd reason sold to the writer Alexei Tolstoy (1882–1945), who for some other odd reason was acquainted with René Malaise from his time in the Soviet Union. What the final transaction looked like was not on record.

What portion of all this was true? Umeå clearly lacked the resources for a closer investigation of the authenticity and provenance of the paintings. They simply had no money for material analysis and X-ray photography, and so the catalogue was based on Malaise's own attributions, even though these were often followed by a tiny qualifying question mark. But did I not sense a certain restrained enthusiasm here and there nevertheless? 'Malaise's own list of the donated works includes several of art history's most prominent names: Mantegna, Zurbaran, Watteau, etc. If these should prove to be correct, the collection is nothing short of sensational.'

In one case, at least, Malaise was guilty of a mistake. It concerned Padovanino's painting of Tarquinius and Lucretia, an imposing work that Malaise supposed to have come to Sweden from Russia after the October Revolution in 1917, but which experts had traced as far back as 1856, at which time it had been hanging in the De Geer family palace in Finspång here in Sweden for many years. But of course that didn't lessen its value.

And Moretto! The treatment of this work in the catalogue grows into a sinuous, Bible-invoking essay on the gentle sensuality and dreamy melancholy of the North Italian Renaissance and becomes a multifaceted homage to the painting, which is of course a copy, but which so captivated Dackenberg that he finally went to Venice to see the original. I can't imagine that Malaise believed in very much beyond himself, but of course he smiled in his heaven as I sat by my computer and read, astonished and delighted, while dusk fell across the islands.

By Sunday morning, I had a clear picture of the situation. René Malaise was an incurable optimist, an adventurer who managed to live both well and long on a meagre diet of pure self-sufficiency and happy calculations worthy of someone in a novel by Balzac. Every time he saw one of his paintings in the Prado or the Louvre or the National Gallery in London, he drew what was for him the obvious conclusion – that the museum had managed to get its hands on a copy. The original, or at least the sketch or first effort, was in his house on Lidingö, an upscale island suburb of Stockholm, and the greatest original of them all was he himself.

But in Malaise's company, you can never be completely certain. He clearly knew a lot and was so audacious that in the summer of 1955 he went to the Eighteenth International Congress of the History of Art in Venice, where he gave a lecture on his Moretto to art experts from the whole world. Yes, he was often wrong, and yes, all his life he willingly let himself be duped. That was easy to see. The hard part is to figure out when he was right. Maybe the thief was the greater expert. I decided to follow a lead that was swept aside decades ago.

. . .

Finding stolen art is difficult, but thanks to the internet it has become a tiny bit easier. The great auction houses put their catalogues on the internet – with pictures and other relevant information – and since I had now seen both the Polack and the Michelangelo in *Collectors' News*, I went into both Bukowski's and Auktionsverket's archives to examine the fine-art auction catalogues of recent years. There was, of course, no Polack, not one, and entering Michelangelo in my search engine seemed merely ridiculous. But once you've started wandering through digital art exhibits, it's hard to stop, so I started poking through the catalogues, one after another, and when I got to the last of them several hours later I'd forgotten what I was looking for. So my surprise was all the greater.

I recognized it immediately. In the Little Bukowski auction catalogue number 157 I saw the same picture I'd seen two days earlier in *Collectors' News*. Item number 225, 'Rembrandt, school of. Oil painting. Old man. Relined canvas, 30 × 25 cm'.

I sat perfectly still for a long time and just stared at the screen, while a short list of stupid questions (What is going on? Is this possible? Why now?) took turns running through my head. The fact was, Little Bukowski's auction number 157 had not yet taken place. It was to be held on Monday, 26 January 2004. The next day.

The article in *Collectors' News*, number 3, 1968, lay open on the table beside my computer. It was titled 'Tales from a Painting's Fate'. I don't know how many times I read it before I finally fell asleep in the wee hours.

The painting shows a man supporting himself on a cane. Malaise caught sight of it in Auktionverket's showrooms on Torsgatan (they moved from those premises in 1961) and thought he knew enough to identify it at once as Dutch, painted in the seventeenth century. But that wasn't all he saw. 'At that period, the brushwork could only be the work of Frans Hals or his pupil Judith Leyster, plus to some extent also the ageing Rembrandt and a few of his students.' Excited by this unexpected find, he went home to study up. The hands and the nose were definitive, he writes. The painter was Frans Hals, without a doubt. 'I was in great suspense when the painting came up for auction the following Monday. It caused no great stir and I was able to acquire it a good deal cheaper than I had anticipated.' So begins the article.

The writer then goes on to develop his theories about the painting. Malaise the entomologist dives enthusiastically into an ocean of esoteric art literature and comes up quickly with the proof he's looking for. True, the painting is not reproduced anywhere, but he finds it nevertheless, in an old German book that refers to an auction in The Hague on 7 October 1771, when a work of Frans Hals went under the hammer – 'a man leaning on a cane' – whose dimensions are given as 29.7 × 24.3 centimetres, which, when checked against actual measurement of the mounted canvas, matches to the millimetre. 'That seemed to settle the question, but then

I happened to see the same painting in the National Gallery in London. The man in this painting was depicted actual size (format 134 × 104 cm) and, although unsigned, it was confidently identified as painted by Rembrandt about 1660.'

So his smaller version is a copy.

But no. At this moment, anyone else would have understood that the curtain had gone down, but not Malaise. He goes on autopilot instead and rolls out a charming little story.

The painting Malaise has purchased is once and for all so masterfully realized that it cannot possibly be a copy. An expert can see this at once. In all probability, he reasons, the National Gallery has got its hands on a copy of his original. And the beauty of it is that their copy may very well have been painted by Rembrandt van Rijn. In broad strokes, the idea is that Frans Hals painted the old man at home in Haarlem, gave the painting to Judith Leyster, who moved to Amsterdam where she installed herself as Rembrandt's mistress (or so Malaise has heard) before later marrying the painter Jan Molenaer. So it is by way of her that the painting made its way to Rembrandt – who found its artistry so exceptionally interesting that he copied it in order to learn a new technique, and because he was an honourable man, he did not sign it. Congrats, London, a genuine Rembrandt! 'Judith Leyster's connection to my painting is based on pure guesswork, of course, but that Rembrandt owned, or at least saw and copied the painting must be considered quite certain.'

Behold the imagination needed to invent a better fly trap!

What remained was the question of why the painting was for sale at just this very moment.

Now it was my turn to theorize. And first of all I turned to the National Gallery, whose most famous works are on the internet for public viewing, including the portrait we're talking about of the old man with the cane. They really were very similar, aside from the size, of course. Of greater importance for my theorizing, however, were two things that had happened since Malaise was in London in the 1960s. In the first place, according to the museum's home page, they had found a signature under the varnish – Rembrandt – and, second, with the help of various sophisticated analyses, they had determined that the painting was a forgery, possibly painted as late as the early eighteenth century.

Did Malaise know that, or suspect it, when he put together his gift to Umeå University? But if that was the case, we can be absolutely certain that he would have forgotten both Hals and Leyster and crafted a completely different and more straightforward history and attribution. Which isn't hard to guess at. Intriguingly, one of the two Rembrandt paintings in Dackenberg's catalogue of the stolen works bore the title 'Portrait of Old Man'. No picture, no measurements. Was that the one to be sold the next day?

And in that case, why? For a good twenty-five years, no one had lifted a finger to shed light on the theft of Malaise's paintings, no one had even bothered about them until I began poking into the whole thing this winter. It couldn't simply be a coincidence. Off the top of my head I could count a number of people who, in light of my researches, had good reason not to have a stolen painting on the wall, if that was what they had. There was no lack of motive.

I decided to go to the auction, more as a spy than a speculator, even though there wasn't much I could possibly learn – I already knew the auction house would refuse to identify the seller. Moreover, I couldn't afford to bid. The minimum bid was listed as 15,000 crowns. But at least I could finally lay eyes on the actual canvas in the flesh, and I could see who bought it.

. . .

I often go to art auctions. It's true that I seldom can afford to buy, but there's something about the atmosphere that makes me prefer them to galleries and museums. I suppose it's the excitement that attracts me.

In any event, when I walked into Bukowski's, down at Nybroplan, this grey, gloomy January Monday, the usual clientele was already assembled, a mixture of dealers and pensioners. It was going to fill up. I was nervous. In order to get a full view of the room and see who bought the portrait, I took a seat furthest back in one corner. It was icy cold. People came and went the entire time, and consequently the door out to Arsenalsgatan was rarely closed. There was a draught.

I'm going to catch cold, I thought, but I stayed where I was for the sake of the view.

Nothing sensational happened. Item number 161, a painting of the Holy Family by an unknown Flemish artist, went for 195,000 crowns, well above the 25,000-crown minimum, but on the whole it was a rather uneventful affair. And draughty, as I mentioned. Finally, I couldn't take it any more and moved further forward in the hall, not far from the table with a green cloth and lots of vases full of tulips where five people were dealing with the telephone bidders. A video camera behind the auctioneer registered the tiniest gesture by any of the numbered paddles. My pulse rose.

Typically, the bidding started at the back. I turned around and tried to see who was bidding, but I was now so poorly located that I couldn't possibly see anything in the crowd of people. Anyway, things were happening. The minimum was quickly surpassed. The bidding continued, now between a person way in the rear and someone on the telephone. The man holding that particular phone was speaking Italian. I watched tensely. Soon only the Italian on the phone was left. Going once. Going twice. Now wait just a minute, I thought, and waved my paddle. And then there was no going back. It was him or me. I mean, was I really going to let René's Rembrandt leave the country? I just couldn't let that happen. The Italian bid 20,000. I waved my paddle until he gave up. The hammer fell. The painting was mine!

. . .

I was now the owner of a copy of a Rembrandt forgery. A small one. Probably stolen. My pulse slowed rapidly, my mouth was dry, I felt a bit dizzy. I stayed in my seat, apathetic in a way, completely empty. The auctioneer's monotone voice on the loudspeaker faded and disappeared. The items being sold did not interest me, nothing interested me any more. I wasn't even cold. I was feeling both nausea and the fear of an oncoming financial problem. Exhausted, I looked out through the tulle curtains in the window, sat there and listened to my own breathing while my gaze wandered over the grey mist and snow in Berzelii Park and on towards the buses and trams at the red lights on Nybroplan and, beyond it, the Royal Dramatic Theatre with its gold filigree, and Sibyllegatan where the Malaise family lived when René was a child, a little way up the slope at number 21.

A memory popped up from somewhere, slowly, like a distant migratory bird in the sudden emptiness. A vague feeling drew closer, a repudiated question and doubt that was somehow associated with this very place and maybe with a play whose title I couldn't remember but that told a story about the curse of poverty, and flight.

There was dialogue. And a singular fragrance.